Ukrainian Daughters' Cookbook

Ukrainian Women's Association of Canada
Daughters of Ukraine Branch,
Regina, Saskatchewan

Ukrainian Daughters' Cookbook
by
Ukrainian Women's Association of Canada
Daughters of Ukraine Branch,
Regina, Saskatchewan

Twelfth Printing – May, 2001

Copyright © 1984 by
Ukrainian Women's Association of Canada
Daughters of Ukraine Branch
1920 Toronto Street
Regina, Saskatchewan   S4P 1M8

Canadian Cataloguing in Publication Data

Main entry under title:

Ukrainian daughters' cookbook

Includes index.
ISBN 0-919845-13-4

I. Cookery, Ukrainian. I. Shiplack, Eunice, 1927-
II. Ukrainian Women's Association of Canada.
Daughters of Ukraine Branch.
TX723.3.U473 1984   641.5947'71   C84-091411-3

Photography by:
Craig Clendening
Camera One
Regina, Saskatchewan

Designed, Printed, and Produced in Canada by:
Centax Books a Division of PW Group
Publishing Director and Food Stylist: Margo Embury
Design by Cynthia Del Rosso
1150 Eighth Avenue
Regina, Saskatchewan, Canada S4R 1C9
(306) 525-2304 FAX: (306) 757-2439
E-mail: centax@printwest.com   www.centaxbooks.com

Ukrainian Women's Association of Canada,
Daughters of Ukraine Branch, Regina, Sask.

Dedication

The Ukrainian Women's Association of Canada, Daughters of Ukraine Branch in Regina humbly dedicate this cookbook to our mothers.

These pioneer women cared enough to instill in us the importance of preserving our Ukrainian culture and traditions.

May this cookbook be a precious resource for us and for future generations.

We wish to thank all the ladies of the Ukrainian Orthodox Cathedral who shared their favorite recipes so generously. Many of the recipes are synonymous with Ukrainians and Ukrainian cooking. We hope you enjoy our Cross-Stitch Designs and Ukrainian Pysanky.

Your Cookbook Committee

Convenor — Eunice Shiplack

Sylvia Bobowsky	Eileen Klopoushak
Marge Dumanski	Rosalyn Monita
Sharon Harras	Rosalie Pankiw
Ann Hneda	Rosalie Prokopchuk
Violet Hubic	Gwen Warnyca

3

Ukrainian Women's Association Daughters of Ukraine Branch, Regina

The women of the Ukrainian Orthodox Church in Canada are united in most congregations into a service group, each group is affiliated with its provincial association and through it with the national federation.

In Regina, the branch is known as Daughters of Ukraine and has a long history. Its founders met February 27, 1927 to plan and organize a branch of the Ukrainian Women's Association. This closely followed the birth of the association, in Saskatoon in December 1926. Though the association now reaches across the nation, the Regina branch was one of its earliest affiliates and gave leadership and example to many others. The first executive was comprised of the founders, Mrs. E. Koziar and Mrs. Miskew, formerly Miss K. Pukesh.

The Daughters of Ukraine determined their aims and objectives after prayerful study. These centred on matters closest to the heart of a Ukrainian Orthdox woman in Canada. They sought to preserve and promote the Orthodox religion and to foster all cultural facets of an old and rich heritage. It included an awareness of the need to involve and inspire their youth to participate in cultural and religious activities. The organization pledged itself to the financial support of the Ukrainian Orthodox Church and its cultural institutions in Canada.

The Regina Branch of the National Association follows the precepts and directives of the parent organization and through participation in provincial and national conferences plays an important part in the formation of policies.

In Regina the membership has its local programs and enjoys a reputation for involvement in community affairs as well as in those pertaining to Ukrainian culture and orthodoxy.

Within the Regina branch, Daughters of Ukraine, there ensued a dual growth of identity — that of being good Ukrainians and Canadians. While promoting good citizenship they resisted assimilation and the loss of their cultural heritage. The dedication and generosity of the members resulted in a quiet spiritual and moral growth leading to an awareness of their destiny. It is their belief that a good Canadian is one who nurtures and preserves his cultural inheritance so that it may enhance the Canadian cultural mosaic.

The association serves as an example of democratic co-operation, of dedication to service and to the Shevchenko determination to retain traditions and religion in an ever encroaching environment. It is our fond hope that young people will continue the work begun in 1926.

Table of Contents

Кишки Кашані

Зварити підгорля, легкі й серце (вепрові) коли на дрібні куски, а росолом, де то все варилося, спарити, наприклад, 4 кварти гречаних круп. Коли не досить, то додати ще кілька ложок смальцю, соли до смаку й двоякого перцю. На покраяне м'ясо вляти кварту крови й добре вимішати. Щоби не було кавалків крови, перетерти м'ясо з кров'ю через друшляк. Змішати з крупами і заки зовсім простигне поначинювати очищені кишки та позавязувати на обох кінцях. Кишки начинювати легко (¾) кишки, класти в широкий баняк в горячу воду і варити повільно через три чверти години. При варенню не прикривати, бо попукають. Пробувати чи готові: проколоти, а як з них виходить чистий сос, то вже зварені. Виняти друшляком, та винести в холодне місце. Коли треба подавати на стіл, відпарити кишки горячою водою, а потім присмажити на свіжім смальци.

Christmas Eve Supper

Свята Вечеря

Sviata Vechera
Traditional Ukrainian Christmas Eve Supper

Twelve different and special dishes are traditional for this meal which begins only after the first star of the evening appears. The twelve dishes are to remind us of the twelve Apostles.

After a day of fasting, in remembrance of the hardships that Mary endured as she and Joseph travelled to Bethlehem, preparations of a spiritual and physical nature set the mood for this Holy Night.

Food for the Holy Supper is prepared with no meat or dairy products. Hay is put under the table and under the tablecloth as a reminder of the humble place of Christ's birth. On top of a white or embroidered tablecloth is placed a Kolach, in the middle of the table. In the middle of the Kolach, a candle is placed which is left burning all night. A lit candle is also placed in the window, to welcome any homeless people. There is always an extra table setting for the souls of the deceased. As dusk approaches, the head of the house brings in a Didukh, a sheaf of grain, and places it near the Icons. As the star appears, the father carries a bowl of Kutia around the home three times, reciting prayers. When all the family is at the table, prayers are recited and the Nativity Tropar is sung, "Boh Predvichny".

The first dish of the twelve is always Kutia, the eldest of the family throws a spoonful of the kutia to the ceiling. The more kernels that stick to the ceiling, the greater the good luck in the following year.

After the completion of the twelve dishes, nuts and candies are scattered in the hay under the table for the children to find. Throughout the rest of the evening, Christmas carols are sung by the family.

When it is almost midnight, all the members of the family go to the Nativity Mass, a celebration of Christ's birth. The traditional greeting is "Khrystos Razdayetsia" (Christ is Born) to which one replies, "Slavite Yoho" (Let us glorify him).

The following day and up to Yordan (Jordan) carollers visit families and friends, starting with the home of the priest, proclaiming the birth of Christ, our Saviour.

The Holy days of the Christmas season end on January 20th "The Feast of St. John the Baptist".

Sviata Vechera

Traditional Dishes for Ukrainian Christmas Eve

Kutia

Kolach

Meatless Borsch

Stuffed Salmon or Fried Fillets

Pickled Herring

Meatless Holubtsi

Varenyky — Potatoes, Sauerkraut or Prunes

Sauerkraut and Peas

Broad Beans or Mashed Beans

Pidpenky with Gravy

Compote

Pampushky, Makiwnyk

Kutia

Kutia is the ritual first dish of the twelve course Christmas Eve Supper. The wheat represents the staff of life. The honey represents the spirit of Christ.

2 cups	wheat	⅓ cup	honey, dissolved in
3 qts.	water		¾ cup hot water
1 cup	poppy seed	½ cup	chopped walnuts,
⅔ cup	sugar		almonds, or
			pecans

Dry wheat in 250°F oven for 1 hour, stir occasionally. Wash, soak in cold water overnight. Next morning, bring wheat to boiling point, simmer 3-4 hours, until kernels burst open.

Scald poppy seed, simmer 3-5 minutes. Drain, grind twice using the finest blade of food chopper. Set aside. Combine honey and sugar in hot water. Set aside. Before serving, add sweetened mixture, poppy seed and nuts to cooled, boiled wheat. See photograph page 18.

Meatless Borsch

3	beets, size of an orange, cut into thin strips	1	large onion, sliced
		3 tbsp.	butter
		1½ cup	cabbage, shredded
1	carrot, diced	1 cup	tomato juice or
8 cups	water		tomato soup
1	medium potato, diced	1½ tbsp.	flour
		½ cup	water, cold
2 tbsp.	lemon juice	2 tbsp.	dill, chopped
½ cup	string beans, green peas, or white beans	½ tsp.	salt
		½ tsp.	pepper

Cook beets and carrots in water for 20 minutes. Add potatoes, simmer 10-15 minutes. Add lemon juice (keeps red colour in beets). Add beans or peas. Simmer until tender.

Sauté onion in butter until soft. Add cabbage to onions with ¼ cup water, simmer until cabbage is tender. Stir into the beets. Add tomato juice or soup. Blend flour with ½ cup cold water, stir into vegetables. Add dill for added flavour. Bring to a boil. Add salt and pepper. Serves 15. See photograph page 18.

Vushka (Tiny Varenyky)

Using a varenyky dough, see page 16, roll out quite thin, cut into 2″ squares. Place a small portion of the mushroom filling on each square of dough, pinch edges together making a triangle, sealing in the filling, now pinch the 2 top ends together again to make it look like an ear (vushka).

Drop vushka into a large pot of boiling salted water. When cooked, they will float to the top, about 10 minutes. Drain in a colander. Pour ¼ cup cooking oil over them and toss well to coat. This will prevent them from sticking. Serve in borsch.

Great for Christmas Eve Supper.

Mushroom Filling:

1	medium onion, chopped	2 cups	mushrooms, sliced
		½ tsp.	salt
3 tbsp.	butter, or oil if using for Christmas Eve	¼ tsp.	pepper
		2	egg yolks

Cook onions in butter. Add mushrooms, salt, and pepper. Cook together about 10 minutes. Turn off heat, cool slightly and beat in egg yolks. Chopped dill may be added for flavor. Cool the mixture thoroughly before filling Vushka.

See photograph page 18.

Kolach

Kolach — a braided ring-shaped bread. The name is derived from the Ukrainian word "kolo" meaning a circle.

1 tbsp.	yeast	¾ cup	butter or margarine, melted
1 cup	lukewarm water		
2 tsp.	sugar	1 tsp.	salt
1 cup	sugar	5	eggs, beaten
4 cups	warm water	12½-13 c.	flour

Dissolve sugar and yeast in water and let stand 10 minutes. Dissolve cup of sugar in 4 cups of warm water. Add melted butter, salt, and beaten eggs. Add yeast mixture. Mix in flour and knead until smooth and elastic. The dough should be just a little stiffer than for bread. Cover, let rise in a warm place until double in bulk. Punch down and let rise again.

Divide the dough into 3 equal pieces. Take ⅓ of the dough and divide into 6 equal pieces. Roll 2 pieces to a length of about 30". Put the 2 lengths side by side, and starting from the centre, entwine dough thus forming a rope-like twist. Do the other half in the same manner. Place the entwined dough in a circle along the edge of a well-greased 9" foil pan. Make 2 more twists about 24" long using the remaining 4 lengths of dough. Now take these 2 twists and entwine them in the opposite direction, making a double twist. Form into a circle. Cut ends at an angle and join neatly by pinching ends together. There should be a small, empty, circular space, in the middle of the pan. See illustration on next page. Let rise to about double in bulk. Be careful not to let the loaves rise too long as the ornaments will lose their definition.

Brush with beaten egg and bake at 350°F for 1 hour.

(Bake Kolach until they sound hollow when bottom is tapped.)

This makes 3 round Kolachi.

See photographs pages 18, 50, and on back cover.

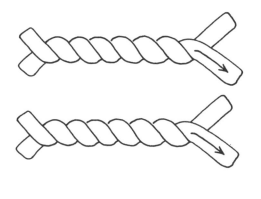

Ornamental Doves

1 cup	boiling water		food color, yellow
1 tsp.	oil	3 cups	flour
1 tsp.	sugar	1	egg, beaten, for glaze
1	egg		

Combine first 5 ingredients. Add 1 cup flour. Mix well with a wooden spoon, then add another 2 cups of flour and knead by hand. If more flour is needed, add a little at a time. The dough is thick, like play dough.

Take a piece of dough, and roll on the table to a pencil shape, about 4″ long. Tie a knot, use the short round end for its head, shape a beak and comb, use poppy seeds for the eyes. Flatten the tail and make about 3 slits with a knife. Bake 15-20 minutes, till beak turns brown. See illustration page 31.

Glaze with well-beaten egg, and return to oven for 5 minutes.

See photographs pages 34 and 66.

To make the Ukrainian wedding bread (Korovai), decorate a Kolach with these ornamental doves and periwinkle.

See photograph on front cover.

Lemon-Rice Stuffed Salmon

5 lb.	salmon	3 tbsp.	lemon juice
1/3 cup	butter	1 tsp.	salt
1 cup	celery, chopped	1/4 tsp.	thyme
1/3 cup	onions, chopped	1/8 tsp.	white pepper
1 1/2 cup	water	1 3/4 cups	rice, uncooked
2 tsp.	lemon rind, grated		

To melted butter add celery and onions and cook until tender. Add remaining ingredients, except rice. Bring to a boil. Add rice, stirring a few times until it returns to a boil. Remove from heat and cover. Let stand 5-10 minutes.

To prepare salmon, season inside and out by rubbing with a cut clove of garlic. Also rub butter over salmon. Season lightly, inside and out, with salt and pepper. Stuff with prepared stuffing, place on well-greased baking dish. Cover with foil.

Bake at 350°F, 10 minutes per pound, plus 10 minutes extra. Garnish with parsley and lemon.

10-12 servings.

See photograph page 18.

Almond Fillets

1/3 cup	flour	1 lb.	perch or sole
1	egg, lightly beaten	4 tbsp.	butter, or oil if
1 tsp.	salt		using for
1/2 cup	fine bread crumbs		Christmas
1/4 cup	almonds, finely		Eve Supper
	chopped		

Measure flour. In separate bowl, combine egg and salt. In third bowl, combine bread crumbs and almonds. Coat fish on both sides with flour, dip into egg mixture, then into crumb mixture.

In large skillet, melt 2 tbsp. butter or oil. Cook fish over medium heat, turning once and adding more butter or oil, until fish flakes easily with fork, about 5-8 minutes.

4 servings.

Pickled Herring

8-10	herrings, medium sized	2 tsp.	pickling spice
1 cup	vinegar	1	bay leaf
3 cups	water	5	onions, sliced
2 tbsp.	sugar	¼ cup	cooking oil

Wash the herring in several waters. Remove the heads, entrails, and tails. Wash again and soak in cold water for 4 hours. Change the water and soak overnight, remove skin and bones if you desire. Cut in pieces. The size depends on the occasion. If you wish, you can leave in large pieces and cut just before serving.

Bring the vinegar, water, sugar, pickling spice, and bay leaf to a boil and cool. Arrange the herring and sliced onions in sealers, cover with the brine and add oil. Let stand 3 days and then serve.

See photograph page 18.

Kapusta (Sauerkraut and Peas)

¾ cup	dried peas	3 tbsp.	flour
3 cups	sauerkraut	1	clove garlic, crushed
¾ cup	water	¼ tsp.	pepper
1	large onion, chopped	½ tsp.	salt
½ cup	oil		

Soak peas overnight. Drain and rinse well. Cover with fresh water and cook until tender. Rinse sauerkraut in water and drain. Add ¾ cup water and cook for 15 minutes. Combine sauerkraut and peas. Reserve liquid.

Sauté onion in oil. Sprinkle flour over onions and brown lightly. Pour reserved liquid into onion mixture, add crushed garlic. Stir until sauce thickens. Add sauce to peas and sauerkraut, stir. Add salt and pepper, simmer for 30 minutes.

See photograph page 18.

Varenyky (Pyrohy)

1½ cup	water	4½ cups	flour
3 tbsp.	cooking oil	1 tsp.	salt
1	egg		

Combine water, cooking oil, and egg, blend well. Then add flour, and salt. Knead dough, adding the last cup of flour, until smooth and soft. Put in a lightly-oiled bowl, and cover. Let dough rest for 20 minutes.

Roll out on a floured board, thinner than for pie crust, and cut out with a round cookie cutter, or into 2 — 2½" squares. Put approximately a tsp. of the filling on it. Fold over forming a half circle and pinch the edges together with the fingers to seal in the filling. Place varenyky on a clean tea towel while making them.

Drop into a pot of boiling water. Do not cook too many at a time. Stir with a wooden spoon a few times to prevent sticking to the bottom. When cooked they will float to the top, about 10 minutes. Remove them with a perforated spoon to a colander and drain thoroughly. Place in a deep dish, sprinkle generously with melted butter, toss very gently to coat the varenyky evenly with butter and prevent them from sticking.

Serve with sour cream or fried chopped onions sautéed in butter until golden. Yield 4 dozen.

Varenyky may be made in large quantity, refrigerated and reheated without any loss of quality.

Place cooked varenyky on a cookie sheet and freeze individually. Next day, put them in plastic bags and keep in freezer. To reheat varenyky, pan-fry in butter until golden color, turn and fry other side.

See photograph page 18.

Varenyky (Pyrohy) Fillings

Potato Filling:

1	medium onion, chopped	½ tsp.	salt
		¼ tsp.	pepper
¼ cup	butter	1 cup	cottage cheese or
3 cups	potatoes, mashed		grated cheese

Sauté onions in butter, add to mashed potatoes. Add salt, pepper, and cottage cheese or grated cheese. Mash well. Cool the mixture thoroughly before placing on varenyky.

Yield about 4 dozen.

Sauerkraut Filling:

1 qt.	sauerkraut	½ tsp.	salt
1	medium onion, chopped	¼ tsp.	pepper
½ cup	oil		

Cook sauerkraut, about 20 minutes or until done. Drain and press out water. Sauté onion in oil until golden. Add sauerkraut, salt, and pepper. Fry for 10 minutes. Cool before putting filling into varenyky. Yield about 4 dozen.

Prune or Plum Filling:

1 cup	prunes or plums	¼ cup	sugar or to taste
½ cup	water		

Boil fruit 20 minutes. Drain and cool. Remove stones and chop finely. Add sugar. Yield, about 1 plum per varenyky.

Poppy Seed Filling:

1 cup	poppy seed	2 tbsp.	sugar
1	egg yolk		

Scald poppy seed. Grind finely. Add egg yolk and sugar. Mix well.

Meatless Holubtsi (Cabbage Rolls)

4 cups	water	1 tsp.	salt
2 cups	rice	½ tsp.	pepper
1	medium onion, finely chopped	4 tbsp.	oil

Cook rice in water according to package instructions, slightly underdone. Sauté the onion in the oil, until transparent. Add the onion to the rice mixture. Stir. Add salt and pepper to taste. Remove from heat. Cool. The mixture is now ready to place into cabbage leaves.

To prepare cabbage:

1	medium-sized cabbage		boiling water
		1 tbsp.	vinegar

Remove core from cabbage. Place cabbage in boiling water to cover. Simmer the cabbage long enough for the leaves to become limp and be easily removed from the head itself. Do not overcook. Remove the leaves from the water, remove the hard centre part of the leaf. The cabbage leaves are now ready to use.

Place a spoonful of rice mixture on the leaf. Roll tightly, closing the ends as you roll each cabbage roll.

Place cabbage rolls in a 2-quart casserole.

¾ cup	tomato juice or	¾-1 cup	tomato soup, diluted with ½ cup water

When baking you may pour tomato juice, stewed tomatoes or tomato soup over the cabbage rolls. Bake at 350°F for 1½-2 hours.

Yield: 20-30 cabbage rolls.

See photograph opposite.

Christmas

1. Kutia (p. 10)
2. Lemon-Rice Stuffed Salmon (p. 14)
3. Pickled Herring (p. 15)
4. Meatless Borsch (p. 10) with Vushka (p. 11)
5. Pidpenky with Gravy (p. 19)
6. Kapusta (Sauerkraut and peas) (p. 15/85)
7. Kolasheny Fasoli (mashed beans) (p. 19)
8. Verenyky (Pyrohy) (p. 16)
9. Meatless Holubtsi (Cabbage Rolls) (p. 18)
10. Yzbap (Compote) (p. 21)
11. Makiwnyk (p. 20)
12. Kolach (p. 12)
13. Pampushky (p. 22)

Pidpenky with Gravy

2 cups	Pidpenky (dried mushrooms)	4 tbsp.	browned flour
		4 cups	hot water
1	large onion, diced	½ tsp.	salt
1	clove garlic, minced	¼ tsp.	pepper
6 tbsp.	oil		

Soak pidpenky overnight. Drain and wash well. Add water to cover pidpenky and boil for 15 minutes. Drain and rinse well. Add water again and boil for 15 minutes. Drain and rinse again. Set aside.

Sauté onion and garlic in oil. Sprinkle browned flour over onion and add 4 cups of hot water. Stir well to make a smooth paste. Add drained pidpenky. Add salt and pepper to taste. Simmer for 15-20 minutes.

If desired, you can fry dill with your onions and garlic.

See photograph page 18.

Mashed Beans

1½ cups	white beans	1 clove	garlic
5 cups	water	1	onion, diced
1 tsp.	salt	2 tbsp.	cooking oil

Pick over the beans, rinse, soak overnight in water to cover. Next day drain, cover with fresh water, boil gently for 1 hour, drain. Cover with 5 cups water and simmer until the beans are tender.

Mash the beans well. Mince 1 garlic clove, and stir into mashed beans. Sauté onion in cooking oil until tender. Sprinkle the onion over the beans. Serve hot.

See photograph page 18.

Makiwnyk

2 tsp.	sugar	1 tsp.	salt
½ cup	water, lukewarm	1½ tsp.	lemon rind,
2 tbsp.	dry yeast		grated
1 cup	milk, lukewarm	1 tsp.	vanilla
	scalded	4-4½ c.	flour
1 cup	flour	2	egg whites, stiffly
8 tbsp.	sugar		beaten
½ cup	butter	1 tbsp.	brown sugar
2	whole eggs, plus	2 tbsp.	water, hot
	2 egg yolks		

Dissolve sugar in lukewarm water. Add the yeast and let stand 10 minutes in warm place. In a large bowl, combine warm milk and 1 cup flour with yeast. Let the sponge rise until bubbles appear, about ½-¾ of an hour. In a separate bowl, beat the sugar and butter until light. Set aside. Beat the eggs together until light and frothy, adding salt. Combine the eggs and the butter-sugar mixture and fold into the yeast. Add lemon rind and vanilla. Add flour and knead until dough feels smooth. Cover and let rise until double in bulk. Punch down and let rise again.

Divide dough into 3 equal parts. Roll each into a rectangular shape about ½" thick. Brush each strip with stiffly beaten egg white, and then spread poppy seed filling over. Roll like jelly roll and seal edges. Place in a greased pan, cover, and let rise in warm place until double in bulk.

Bake in 350°F oven for 15 minutes, lower heat to 300°F, and bake another 40-50 minutes. Brush immediately with a syrup made with brown sugar dissolved in hot water. Cool before cutting.

Continued on page 21.

Poppy Seed Filling:

1 cup	poppy seed	½ cup	chopped walnuts
⅓ cup	sugar	1	egg white, stiffly
1 tsp.	lemon rind, grated		beaten

Scald poppy seed, drain. Cover with warm water and soak for 30 minutes. Drain thoroughly. Grind fine. Mix with sugar, rind, nuts, and stiffly beaten egg white.

See photograph page 18.

Compote

1 lb.	dried apricots	5	whole cloves
1 lb.	mixed dried fruits	10 cups	water
½ lb.	pitted, prunes	1 cup	granulated sugar or
1 cup	golden raisins		1 cup honey may
1	lemon, sliced or		be used
	1 orange, sliced	¼ cup	brandy or orange
2	cinnamon sticks		liqueur (optional)

Place all dried fruits, lemon, cinnamon, and cloves in a non-aluminum saucepan.

Add water, cover, and let stand for 4 hours or overnight.

Add sugar, bring to a boil and simmer, covered, until fruit is tender, about 10 minutes. Taste, adding sugar or honey, if desired. Let cool slightly. Add brandy, if desired.

12 to 16 small servings.

Note: You may use your own combination of dried fruits.

See photograph page 18.

Pampushky

2 tbsp.	yeast	3	eggs
2 tsp.	sugar	4	egg yolks
1 cup	water, lukewarm	1 tsp.	vanilla
1 cup	water, warm	6½ cups	flour (enough to
1 cup	scalded milk		make a soft dough)
2 cups	flour	¾ cup	sugar
¾ cup	butter or oil	1 tsp.	salt

Dissolve yeast and sugar in one cup of lukewarm water. Then add 1 cup water, scalded milk and 2 cups of flour. Beat until smooth. Cover bowl and put in warm place to rise until light and bubbly.

Cream butter and sugar, add eggs and yolks, salt and vanilla. Beat till light. Combine first mixture and knead to a soft dough. Add flour, mix well and knead. Allow to rise till double in bulk. Punch down and let it rise again. Roll out on floured board, cut with round cookie cutter. Place a tsp. of filling in each piece and seal edges. Place pampushky, seal down, on a clean tea towel. Allow to rise, then fry in Mazola oil.

Poppy Seed Filling:

2 cups	poppy seed	4 tbsp.	honey
1	egg white	1 tsp.	cinnamon
½ cup	sugar		

Boil poppy seed for ½ hour. Drain. Let stand 1 hour, then put through the finest blade of food chopper. Add egg white, sugar, honey, and cinnamon. Mix well.

See photograph page 18.

Easter

Великдень

Ukrainian Easter

Easter, the most glorious and radiant event in all history, commemorates the resurrection of Christ.

With the ringing of the church bells at midnight on Saturday, the joyful Easter Matins begin. The triumphant resurrection service begins with a procession around the church. Temporarily, the darkened church is emptied and the doors are closed, representing the closed tomb of Christ. The procession circles the church three times, symbolizing the journey of the myrrh-bearing women to the tomb of Christ in the early hours of the morning to anoint his body.

The visit to the empty sepulchre by the women is climaxed when the risen Saviour is seen and recognized. Here the priest greets the worshippers with the traditional words, "Christ is Risen". The people respond with "He is indeed Risen". The church bells peal, the worshippers re-enter the church and the Easter service proceeds to its joyful completion. The royal gates are kept open the entire Easter week to symbolize that the gates of Heaven have been opened to all faithful believers.

It is the custom to exchange or give Easter eggs (Pysanky) with the Easter greeting, "Krystos Voskres" to which the reply is "Voistyno Voskres".

Immediately after the service, people return home to break the long fast with an Easter breakfast of consecrated or blessed food. The menu consists of boiled eggs, a variety of hot and cold meats, roast suckling pig, cheese, salads, horseradish and beet relish, and delectable Easter breads and pastries. The meal begins with Easter grace, followed by a ceremonious serving of the blessed egg, which the elder head of the family divides into portions, one for each person, again with the greeting of Easter. This ritual symbolizes family unity and expresses hope for a happy and prosperous year until next Easter.

Sviachene

Traditional Foods for the Blessing of the Easter Baskets

hard-boiled eggs

meat products — ham, roast pork, lamb

sausage — Kowbasa

butter

cheese or egg-cheese

fresh horseradish root

salt

Paska, Babka

Pysanky

The Easter Dinner would include all of the above Blessed Foods, plus a selection of the following:

Holubtsi

mashed potatoes — gravy

Pyrohy

vegetables

salads

Studenetz

tortes or cheesecakes

beverages

Perfect Hard-Boiled Eggs

Cover desired amount of eggs with cold water in an appropriate-sized pot. Bring to a boil, turn off heat, cover pot and let stand for about ½ hour. Run cold water over eggs to cool.

Eggs will be properly hard-boiled without grey rings.

See photograph page 34.

Saltseson

2	pork hocks	1	pork tongue
½	small pork head	1	pig's stomach
2	pig's ears	2	celery stalks
1	pork heart	1	medium onion

Scrub and wash very thoroughly hocks, head and ears. Remove the veins and arteries from the heart, and wash thoroughly. Soak all meat overnight in salted water.

Scrub and wash tongue. Boil tongue until tender, discard stock. Peel skin off, cut into long strips ½'' wide. Set aside.

Clean and wash pig's stomach very thoroughly.

In a large kettle, place all meat. Cover with water and bring to a boil. Skim off foam and add celery and onion. Cover and simmer until meat falls away from bones. Remove vegetables, separate the meat from the bones, and chop into bite-sized pieces. Cut skins and ears into ½'' to ¼'' wide strips. Combine the meat and tongue, mix well.

Add to the combined meat:

4-5 cups	pork stock	3	cloves garlic crushed
½ tsp.	pepper	2 tbsp.	salt

Mix well; fill stomach about ¾ full with meat mixture and sew the edges securely. Place saltseson on rack in large pot; cover completely with hot water; simmer, for 1 hour. Prick with needle, if done juice will run clear. Remove from roaster, when cool. Place a weighted board on top to flatten slightly, allow to set overnight.

A delicious pressed loaf; an old country delicacy.

Ukrainian Sausage

30 lbs.	ground meat	2 tsp.	pepper
	(⅔ beef, ⅓ pork)	⅔ cup	tenderquick salt
2 cups	flour	¼ cup	salt
9 tbsp.	sausage seasoning	½ cup	garlic, crushed
1 tsp.	nutmeg	5 cups	warm water
1 tsp.	oregano		

Method:

Mix all ingredients well and let stand overnight so that seasonings will blend together. In the morning mix one more time and then fill the casings (fills approximately ½ lb. of casings).

Hang sausages and smoke them (using willows or oak) for at least 6 hours. They will now be ready to eat.

See photograph page 50.

Honey-Glazed Ham

6 lb.	country-style ham	2 tbsp.	honey
	whole cloves	3 tbsp.	brown sugar

Put ham into large bowl, cover with water and let soak overnight. Next day, drain the ham. Place it in a large saucepan and cover with fresh water. Bring to a boil. Remove any scum. Reduce heat, cover, and simmer for 1½ hours.

Preheat the oven to 350°F. Remove ham from pan, allow to cool slightly, then cut off any rind. Score fat in a lattice pattern and put a clove in the center of each "diamond".

Gently heat brown sugar and honey in a small saucepan until melted. Brush over the surface of the ham. Put ham in a roasting pan and cook in the oven for 30 minutes, basting from time to time. Take care not to let the glaze burn. 10 servings.

See photograph page 34.

Studenetz

3	pigs feet	1	clove garlic
3	pork hocks	1	bay leaf
2 tbsp.	Morton salt	2 tbsp.	Morton salt
1	medium onion, sliced thinly	1	clove garlic

Cut pigs feet in half lengthwise, soak hocks and pigs feet in cold water and 2 tablespoons of salt overnight. Drain, then scrape and wash hocks and feet thoroughly. Place the meat in a large kettle, add 2 tablespoons Morton salt, cover with cold water and bring to boil. Skim, add onion, garlic, and bay leaf then simmer very slowly without a cover. This is very important, rapid boiling will make broth milky. Continue to boil slowly until meat comes off bones easily. Separate the meat from the bones, chop to desired cubes. Place in oblong glass pans. Crush 1 clove of garlic and add to juice and stir, then strain juice through sieve over chopped meat, stir slightly and chill thoroughly. Before serving scrape fat off top and serve in slices or squares.

See photograph page 50.

Easter Horseradish

1 cup	fresh horseradish, ground	¼ cup	honey, room temperature
2 tbsp.	soft butter, room temperature	6-8	hard-cooked eggs

Combine horseradish, butter, and honey.

Mash eggs, add to the horseradish mixture. Mix well. More eggs could be added for a milder horseradish taste.

This dish is excellent served with eggs, sausage, beef, or even pork.

Horseradish Sauce

4 cups	finely grated horseradish	1 tsp.	salt
3 cups	sugar	3 tbsp.	flour
2 cups	sweet cream	1¼ cups	vinegar
3 cups	milk	4	eggs, well-beaten

Mix above ingredients well. Cook till it comes to a boil — stirring constantly. Simmer for 15 to 20 minutes. Put in jars and seal.

Easter Cheese and Butter

Cheese for the basket for blessing can be either simple cottage cheese or cream cheese. Cream cheese or egg-cheese can be formed into an egg-shape; cream cheese should be at room temperature and could be shaped by first softening then placing on a sheet of plastic wrap and moulding the wrapped cheese with your hands into an egg shape.

A simple decoration for cheese or butter is to form a cross on the top using whole cloves.

See photograph page 34.

Easter Macaroni Casserole

2½ cups	egg noodles	½ tsp.	salt
½ cup	butter, melted	¼ tsp.	cinnamon
½ cup	raisins, well-washed	3	eggs, beaten
¼ cup	sugar	1 cup	scalded milk, cooled

Cook noodles in salted water until almost done. Drain well. Add melted butter and mix well. Add raisins. Mix sugar, salt, cinnamon, beaten eggs, and milk and add to macaroni. Place in well-buttered casserole and bake in a moderate oven, 350°F, for 30 minutes or until golden brown on top.

Easter Paska

Easter Paska is a work of art produced especially for the blessing of the basket of foods at the church. The Paska is made with eggs, butter, and other good things to produce a fine, rich loaf, appropriate for the importance of this special bread.

The Paska in the Easter basket reminds us that Christ is the Living Bread. Pride is taken in the ornamentation that decorates the top of the Paska — crosses, twists, rosettes, pine cones.

½ cup	warm water	1 tsp.	sugar
1½ tbsp.	yeast		

Combine until yeast is dissolved, 10 minutes.

6	eggs, beaten	1 tsp.	salt
½ cup	white sugar	3 cups	lukewarm water
½ cup	butter	10-11 c.	flour
½ cup	oil		

Combine the softened yeast with beaten eggs, add sugar, butter, oil, salt, and water. Mix in the flour and knead until smooth and elastic. The dough should be just a little stiffer than for bread. Cover, let rise in a warm place until double in bulk. Punch down and let rise again.

Take dough, make a round base 1″ thick, and cover the bottom of a round 9″ greased pan.

Take 2 equal-sized pieces of dough, roll each to 36″ lengths. Place side by side and starting from centre, entwine each about the other, do the other half in the same manner, place the entwined length on the base, in a circle along the edge. Roll 4 equal pieces of dough each to 10″ lengths, entwine 2 lengths on the base to cross each other at the centre, curl each end. Let rise to almost double in bulk.

Be careful not to let the paska rise too long, as the ornaments will lose their definition. Brush lightly with beaten egg. (Formerly, a feather brush was used for this delicate task.) Bake in 325°F oven for 15 minutes then bake 45 minutes at 350°F. See photograph page 34.

Makes 3 or 4 paska.

Easter Doves

In Ukraine, in early times, the return of the birds in the spring was celebrated with special spring songs. Birds made of dough were also baked, representing larks who were migrating back to the north. Today these bread "doves" are made for Easter. Save some of your Paska dough to make them or see recipe page 13. See illustrations below.

See photographs pages 34, 66 and on front cover.

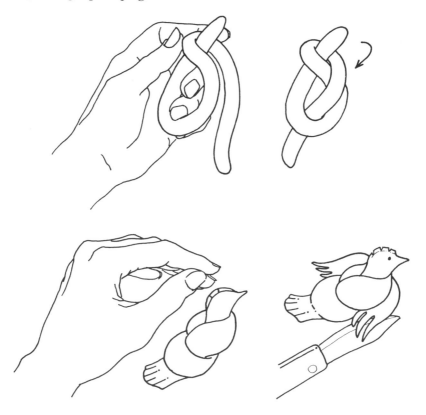

Easter Babka

This rich bread is traditionally served at Easter. The name "baba" in Ukrainian means "grandmother" or "woman" and the diminutive form is "babka".

2 tbsp.	yeast	1 cup	warm water
1 tbsp.	sugar		

Combine until yeast is dissolved, 10 minutes.

2 cups	milk, scalded	1 tsp.	salt
9-9½ c.	flour	¼ tsp.	mace
10	egg yolks	½ lb.	butter, melted
5	egg whites	1 tbsp.	orange rind, grated
1 cup	sugar	1 cup	raisins

To dissolved yeast, add 1 cup warm milk and 1 cup flour. Beat with wire whisk till smooth. Let rise in warm place till bubbles appear, about 1 hour.

Beat yolks, then add sugar and beat till lemony colour, add salt, mace and rind.

Add half the butter and the second cup of milk and 3 cups of flour. Beat thoroughly, adding the yeast mixture and stiffly beaten egg whites.

Add rest of flour to make soft dough, kneading for ½ hour and adding the rest of the butter and raisins. Let rise in warm place till double in bulk. Punch down and let rise again.

Prepare tins (2 or 3 lb. coffee cans) by greasing with lard and sprinkling lightly with very fine bread crumbs.

Shape dough into round balls with smooth top and place in tin, using up ⅓ of the space. Let rise in warm place till reaches top.

Brush top with beaten egg and bit of milk, taking care to wipe away any egg at rim of tin, to prevent catching dough, which holds it from rising.

Bake at 350°F for 15 minutes, then 300°F for another hour. When baked, let stand in tins for 4-5 minutes. Then carefully remove and place on soft surface, a folded soft blanket or cushion, turning them over after 10 or 15 minutes to avoid denting.

See photograph pages 34 and 66.

Easter Babka

3 tbsp.	yeast	1 cup	sugar
1 tsp.	sugar	1 tsp.	salt
½ cup	water		grated rind of
2 cups	scalded milk,		1 lemon
	cooled	1	orange, juice of
½ lb.	melted butter	1 tsp.	vanilla (optional)
10	yolks and 2 whole	9-10 c.	flour
	eggs, well-beaten	1 cup	raisins

Combine yeast and sugar in water. Let stand for 10 minutes. Add yeast to the remaining ingredients, adding flour and raisins last to make very soft dough.

Let rise. When doubled in bulk, punch down and let rise again. Put in greased pans (let rise). Bake at 325°F for ¾ to 1 hour, depends on size of pans. Makes 4-5 loaves.

See photographs pages 34 and 66.

Cheesecake

Crumb Mixture:

⅓ cup	melted butter	3 tbsp.	sugar
1½ cups	graham wafer crumbs	¾ tsp.	cinnamon

Combine all ingredients. Press ⅔ of crumb mixture into greased 9'' springform pan (or other round pan with deep sides). Chill until set.

Cake Mixture:

2 cups	dry cottage cheese	4	eggs, separated
½ cup	sugar	3 tbsp.	flour
2 tsp.	lemon juice	⅔ cup	light cream
	Rind of 1 lemon, grated	¼ tsp.	cream of tartar
¼ tsp.	salt		

Mix cottage cheese, ¼ cup sugar, lemon juice, lemon rind, and salt by hand or with mixer at medium speed for 10 minutes. Blend in 4 egg yolks. Mix in flour and cream and beat at medium speed for 3 minutes.

In a separate bowl beat egg whites until frothy. Add cream of tartar and remaining ¼ cup sugar. Beat until peaks form. Fold cheese mixture into egg white. Pour into crumb-lined pan. Sprinkle remaining crumbs on top.

Bake at 300°F, for 1 hour. Turn off heat and let cake stand in oven for 1 hour. Remove cake from oven, let stand 5 minutes. Remove from pan.

Serves: 12.

See photograph page 130.

ХРИСТОС
ВОСКРЕС

Easter

1. Easter Paska (p. 30)
2. Babka (p. 32/33/66)
3. Easter Cottage Cheese (p. 29)
4. Salt
5. Easter Butter (p. 29)
6. Perfect Hard-Boiled Eggs (p. 26)
7. Ukrainian Sausage (p. 27)
8. Honey-Glazed Ham (p. 27)
9. Kyshka (Buckwheat Sausage) (p. 51)
10. Easter Doves (p. 13/31)

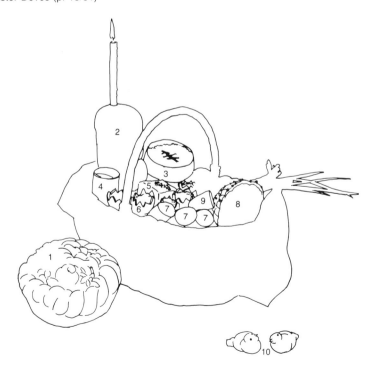

Unbaked Cheese Paska

2 lbs.	dry curd cheese	¾ cup	whipping cream
¾ cup	unsalted butter, softened	½ tsp.	salt
		1 tsp.	vanilla
1½ cups	icing sugar	½ cup	raisins, finely chopped or
4	egg yolks		
1	egg, boiled and put through sieve		1 cup drained crushed pineapple

Mold — one 6'' plastic flower pot with a hole at the bottom. Line the pot with a dampened cheesecloth of double thickness.

Press cheese through sieve, or mix in blender until smooth. Cream butter and sugar until light. Beat in egg yolks, 1 at a time. Press yolk-creamed mixture through sieve. Combine with cheese.

Pour mixture into prepared mold. Cover with cheesecloth and place a saucer on top, with a weight on it, so the juice can drain out.

Chill in refrigerator at least 24 hours. Unmold on plate and garnish with fresh strawberries, pineapple, or grapes before serving.

Replace mold on top to store in refrigerator.

Pysanky (Easter Eggs)

The egg, symbolizing the rebirth of nature, is known to have been used in the early pre-Christian ceremonies during the celebration of the spring festival. With the advent of Christianity this symbolism was interpreted to mean man's rebirth. The egg was thus given a new meaning and was incorporated into the celebration of the Resurrection of Christ.

There are many legends centred around pysanky. One such legend is that, as long as Easter eggs are decorated, good will prevail over evil.

Pysanky play an important part in traditional Ukrainian Easter customs. The eggs are placed in the Easter basket which is taken to be blessed during the Easter Sunday church service. After the eggs have been blessed they are believed to contain talismanic powers. The eggs are exchanged with friends, presented as gifts and used as decorations year round.

There are various types of Easter eggs, the two most widely known are the "pysanky" and "krashanky". The word "pysanka" (singular) is derived from the word "pysaty" which means "to write"; "pysanky" being the plural form. "Krashanky" are hard-cooked, solid-coloured eggs and, unlike the pysanky, these are made to be eaten. Krashanka is derived from the word "kraska" meaning "colour". These eggs are also placed in the Easter basket to be blessed and are traditionally the first food eaten, to break the fast, following Lent.

The many different patterns used on the eggs have been handed down from generation to generation. The various regions of Ukraine have patterns particular to that region. However, there are patterns which are common to many regions.

In decorating the "pysanka" one should keep in mind the symbolic meaning of the motifs being used. The motifs used are generally classified in three categories: animal, plant, and geometric.

See photographs pages 34 and 98.

Geometric Motifs

Geometric motifs are the oldest and most widely used form of decoration. Examples of these are triangles, ribbons or belts, stars, crosses and circles.

Dots are frequently used and may be small or large. These are at times scattered over the entire field of the design to suggest stars or may also represent Mary's tears.

The triangle is widely used. This is an ancient symbol which symbolizes any trio; i.e. air, fire, and water and more recently the Holy Trinity. The pysanka known as "The Forty Days of Lent" is divided into forty triangles, which represent the forty days and nights Jesus Christ spent fasting.

Ribbons, belts, and lines encircling the egg with no beginning or end are called the "endless lines", symbolizing eternity.

The six or eight point star or rose and circles of various sizes are symbols of the sun. These signify happiness, protection from harm, well-being, and good fortune.

Plant Motifs

The whole plant or parts are often drawn on the egg. These motifs do not represent the plant in natural detail but rather are stylized versions of the plant.

The "pine tree" motif can be drawn in many combinations. It is sometimes placed in the form of a cross. Pinetree motifs symbolize everlasting life and youth.

The tree is drawn with fine lines extending from a trunk to depict branches. Trees symbolize the "Tree of Life" or strength.

Other popular plant motifs are periwinkles, oak leaves, grapes, wheat, and pussy willows.

Animal Motifs

The animal motif dates back to ancient times. The more common animals depicted on pysanky are deer, horses, fish, butterflies, birds, and hens. At times only parts of the animals are drawn, e.g. ram's horns, hen's feet, or duck's feet. The hen symbolizes fertility, the deer, wealth and prosperity.

Colours

The colours used to decorate the eggs also have symbolic meaning. For example, white symbolized purity and innocence; red — passion, spirituality, and bravery; yellow — good harvest; black — remembrance.

Materials Required to Make Pysanky

Eggs — Select clean white eggs free of blemishes and cracks. The eggs should have a hard shell and be symmetrical. Fresh farm eggs which have not been washed are preferred.

If eggs require some washing this should be done using a vinegar-water solution (suggest two tablespoons vinegar to one quart water). Gently wash the egg in this solution. Do not rub. Pat dry with a clean cloth or tissue.

Eggs should be at room temperature before they are used, or problems will arise during application of the wax. Traditionally, the eggs are used in the raw state. Boiling the eggs tends to remove the natural oils from the shell; this results in the dyes not taking as well.

Beeswax — The unique characteristics of beeswax make it suitable for writing pysanky. Paraffin wax cannot be substituted. The dyes used will not penetrate or cling to areas which were covered with beeswax. For safety reasons, one should realize that beeswax is flammable and will cling to one's skin.

Dyes — The dyes generally sold for making pysanky are chemical dyes and thus are inedible.

Prepare the dyes as directed on the package. Make your dyes well in advance of using them, as they should be used at room temperature. Dyes should be made in clean, wide-mouthed jars which have tight-fitting lids.

Four basic colours are all that are needed by the beginner, yellow, orange, bright red, and black. Other colours such as green, blue, dark red, turquoise, purple, and brown are available, and can be used as one gains more experience, and wants to broaden one's patterns.

Kistka — The writing instrument used to apply the beeswax to the egg is called a kistka. The kistka is made by attaching a small metal cone, usually brass, to a stick. These can be purchased ready-made in various sizes from Ukrainian speciality stores or hobby shops.

It is advisable to have kistky on hand that have different-sized openings. A variety of sizes will permit one to draw fine lines or fill in large areas with wider lines.

Electric kistky are also available. These allow the writer to make more uniform lines and work somewhat faster.

Other Materials

Candle — used to heat the kistka. Candle should be held securely in a proper holder.

Pencil — may be used to outline the egg patterns before commencing wax application.

Spoons — one for each colour, used when placing the egg in and removing it from the dye.

Toothpicks — to apply dye to those spaces in the design which call for only small touches of a colour. This is often the method used for such colours as green and blue.

Razor Blade — to scrape off wax in event of an error.

Paper Towels — to dry eggs after they have been taken from the dye.

Clean soft cloth — used to wipe egg when beeswax is removed.

Vinegar — used in cleaning eggs or can be used to strengthen the dyes if they begin to weaken.

Method for Writing an Easter Egg

Before beginning be sure your hands are clean and free of hand creams. The egg may be held in a tissue or rested on the table top on a clean paper towel when working.

Divide the egg into the basic lines as illustrated. Hold the pencil steady at the top of the egg and rotate the egg to make a continuous line lengthwise on the egg. Draw another line at right angles to the first again beginning at the top. The egg is now divided into quarters — Figure 1.

Next draw a line horizontally around the middle of the egg. The egg is now divided into 8 equal parts — Figure 2.

Remember never to erase pencil marks from the egg as the dyes will not adhere well to the areas erased.

Beginning at the centre draw diagonal lines so that each side of the egg is divided into 8 sections — Figure 3.

The basic lines are now complete. The wax can now be applied.

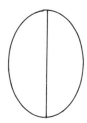 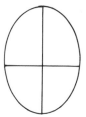 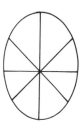

Heat the tip of the kistka (metal cone) in the candle flame and press the heated tip into the cake of beeswax. Working quickly draw over all the pencil lines with beeswax. Best results will be obtained if the kistka is kept at right angles to the egg when writing. Remember again to rotate the egg in order to get a smooth even line. The process of heating the kistka and pressing it into the wax will be repeated several times before all the lines are drawn as the beeswax cools quickly.

When dyeing the eggs be sure not to leave them in too long (hours) as the dyes will seep into the egg shell and seep under the succeeding dyes and wax, thus ruining the egg design.

Apply the wax in each of the eight sections on each side of the egg to get the star design — Figure 4.

Next dip the egg into the yellow dye. Remove the egg when it has reached the desired colour and pat dry with paper towelling.

On the yellow egg apply wax to those lines as shown in Figure 5.

Next dye the egg orange and pat dry. Wax in those lines as shown in Figure 6.

The egg is next dyed red. Pat dry. Using a kistka giving a thicker line fill in the star points solidly with wax, being sure that no spots have been left unwaxed — Figure 7.

The final step is dying the egg black. Pat dry. Allow the egg to dry at least 15 minutes before the wax is removed.

There are various ways to remove the wax. It can be removed by very carefully moving the egg through the *side* of the candle flame until the wax begins to shine. Wipe the softened wax off with a soft clean cloth. Continue working in small areas of the egg until the wax has been removed from the entire egg. Be sure not to hold the egg in the top of the flame as soot will collect on the egg and ruin your design.

If a large number of eggs are to have the wax removed, these may be placed in an oven that has been preheated to 180-200°F. Leave the eggs in the oven approximately 20 minutes or until they take on a wet appearance. Remove the eggs one at a time and wipe off the wax with a clean, soft cloth. Set cleaned eggs in a carton or bowl to cool.

To give the eggs a hard glossy finish they can be coated with a clear gloss liquid plastic (Varathane). This is applied by dipping a finger into the Varathane and spreading a thin layer over the entire egg. The egg is then placed on an egg rack to dry. The egg rack can be constructed by pounding nails into a board in such a way that they will hold an egg — Figure 8.

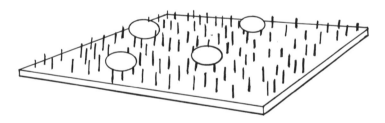

The contents of the eggs will eventually dry out. To ensure that they dry out evenly they should be turned over every few months. The eggs should be kept in a well ventilated place to facilitate drying and to avoid over heating, which can lead to cracking and exploding.

Traditional Foods

Традиційні Страви

Kapusnyak (Sauerkraut Soup)

2 lbs.	spare ribs (fresh)	3 cups	sauerkraut
8 cups	water	½ cup	rice
1	medium onion, chopped	½ tsp.	salt
		¼ tsp.	pepper
1	large potato, diced	1	bay leaf
1	carrot, shredded		chopped parsley

Wash the meat, cover with water, add onion, and bay leaf, simmer until meat is tender. More water should be added as it evaporates. Add rice, potato, carrot, and sauerkraut, continue simmering until vegetables are done (20 minutes or so).

Garnish with parsley.

Meat may be served as separate course or cut into small pieces and served in soup. This soup is usually eaten with rye bread.

See photograph page 50.

Eileen's Borsch

3	medium potatoes, diced	3-4	carrots
1	medium onion, chopped	2	medium potatoes diced (second) amount)
½	medium cabbage, shredded	10 oz.	can tomato soup salt, pepper
⅓ cup	butter		dill, parsley

Cook the 3 potatoes in 6 cups salted water. When well done, mash the potatoes in the water. In the meantime, fry onions and cabbage in butter. Add to soup base. Simmer. Add diced carrots and potatoes. Then add tomato soup. Simmer until carrots and potatoes are cooked. Season to taste with salt, pepper, dill and parsley.

Even better the next day.

Deep-Fried Varenyky (Pyrohy)

1 cup	water	½ tsp.	soda
½ cup	oil	½ tsp.	salt
1	egg	3 cups	cottage cheese
3-3½ c.	flour		pressed through sieve

Combine water, cooking oil, and egg, blend well. Then add 2 cups of flour, cottage cheese, soda and salt. Knead dough, adding the last cup of flour, until smooth and soft. Put in a slightly-oiled bowl and cover. Let dough rest for 20 minutes.

On a floured board, roll out dough, thinner than for pie crust, and cut out circles with a round cookie cutter. Put approximately a teaspoonful of the filling on dough, fold over, forming a half circle, and pinch the edges together with your fingers, to seal in the filling. Place varenyky on a clean tea towel when making them.

Fry in hot cooking oil, 375°F, for about 3 minutes until golden, turning them over to fry on the other side. Drain on absorbent paper. Serve with sour cream, or fried chopped onions.

Yield: 6 dozen.

Varenyky may be made in a large quantity and frozen. To reheat varenyky, pan-fry varenyky in butter, turn and fry other side. Cottage cheese may be frozen to give it a fine texture, so sieving is not necessary.

Varenyky filling on page 17.

See photograph page 50.

Baked Pyrizhky

1½ tbsp.	yeast	1 cup	warm water
1 tbsp.	sugar		

Dissolve sugar and yeast in warm water.

4	eggs, beaten	¼ cup	butter, add to hot
½ cup	oil		milk and cool
1 tsp.	salt	1 cup	warm water
1 cup	milk, scalded	2 tbsp.	sugar
		8 cups	flour, approximately

Beat eggs, oil, salt, add yeast mixture and the rest of ingredients. Add flour, knead to a soft dough. Let rise for 1 hour. Make little balls, the size of a walnut, let rest a few minutes. Stretch with your fingers, put filling in, seal. Let rise ¾ hour and bake at 350°F until golden.

Serve with Cream Sauce With Dill.

Filling:

3 lbs.	potatoes	2 tbsp.	dill
1 lb.	yellow cheese or	2 tbsp.	green onion, chopped
	cottage cheese		

Cook and mash potatoes. Add cheese, dill, and onion.

Cream Sauce With Dill:

2	green onions,	1 cup	whipping cream
	chopped		dill
2 tbsp.	butter		
1 tbsp.	flour		

Fry onions in the butter for 2 minutes, add flour, stir and cool for 1 minute. Bring cream to a boil until it thickens, add dill and onions (as much as desired). Serve over Pyrizhky.

Makes approximately 4 dozen. These Pyrizhky freeze well.

See photograph page 50.

Homemade Noodles

| 12 | eggs | 1 tsp. | salt |
| 1 cup | warm water | 11-12 c. | flour |

Beat eggs with electric beater. Add water, mix with flour and salt and knead well. This makes a stiff dough. Put in bowl, cover tightly and let dough rest for 30 minutes, as this makes the dough easier to work with. Put dough through a noodle machine or roll out to almost paper-thin and allow it to dry partially. Turn the dough over in order to dry the other side slightly. It must be neither sticky nor dry and brittle. Fold into a long roll, cut the roll crosswise into fine shreds. Spread them out to dry. The noodles may be used at once or dried thoroughly and stored. May also be frozen.

When ready to use, drop in large quantity of boiling salted water. Stir and cook about 8 minutes. Drain in a colander and rinse with cold water to prevent sticking. Use as required.

Baked Millet Kasha

1 cup	millet	1 tbsp.	onion, chopped, fried
3 cups	cream or rich milk	1 tsp.	salt
½ cup	butter	½ tsp.	sugar

Wash millet until the water is clear, drain well.

Boil cream, add millet and cook until thickened. Remove from heat, add butter, onion, salt, and sugar. Mix. Pour into a casserole dish and bake at 325°F for 50-60 minutes.

Serve with creamed cottage cheese and baked ham.

Bukovinian Nachinka

6	slices bacon	1 tsp.	salt
1	small onion, finely chopped	¼ tsp.	pepper
		1 tsp.	sugar
3 tbsp.	butter or bacon drippings	3½ cups	milk, scalded
		3	eggs, well-beaten
1 cup	cornmeal	½ cup	light cream

Fry bacon until crisp. Add onion and sauté. Remove bacon and onion. Bacon drippings can be used instead of butter. On low heat, gently stir in the cornmeal and stir so it is coated. Add salt, pepper, and sugar.

Scald milk and add it gradually, stirring constantly, until bubbly and all the milk is gone. Simmer until thickened.

Remove from heat and add eggs, cream, bacon pieces, and onion. Fold gently. Pour into 2 quart casserole and bake uncovered in oven for 1 hour at 350°F.

Nachinka

(serves 100 people)

1 cup	diced onion	⅓ cup	sugar
1 lb.	butter	2 tbsp.	salt
6 cups	cornmeal	2 tsp.	pepper
6 qts.	milk	24	eggs
4 cups	cream	4 tsp.	baking powder

Sauté onions in butter. Add cornmeal and fry for a little longer. Combine milk, cream, sugar, salt, and pepper. Heat until warm, add to cornmeal, mixing constantly. Let cook till thickened (if lumpy beat with egg beater). Remove from heat and add well-beaten eggs and baking powder. Fold in gently. Pour into large greased roasting pan. Bake uncovered at 350°F for 1-1½ hours, or until golden brown.

Traditional

1. Ukrainian Sausage (p. 27)
2. Ukrainian Sausage and Sauerkraut (p. 51)
3. Nalysnyky (p. 54)
4. Studenetz (p. 28)
5. Beets and Horseradish
6. Nachinka (p. 52)
7. Baked Pyrizhky (p. 48)
8. Varenyka (Pyrohy) (p. 16)
9. Deep-Fried Varenyky (p. 47)
10. Kolach (p. 12)
11. Kapusnyak (Sauerkraut Soup) (p. 46)
12. Holubtsi (p. 18/52)
13. Korzi z Makom (p. 55)
14. Various Braided Breads see Kolach recipe (p. 12)

Kyshka (Buckwheat Sausage)

2 lb.	pork riblets	¼ tsp.	pepper
4 qts.	water	2 lbs.	whole buckwheat
1	bay leaf	2 lbs.	fresh pork, ground
2	whole onions	2 cups	fresh blood
½ tsp.	salt	6	beef casings

Boil riblets in water till meat is tender. (Bay leaf, onions, salt, and pepper are added to the water while meat is cooking.)

Dry buckwheat in an oven, 300°F for 45 minutes. Brown freshly ground pork. Add meat from cooked riblets. Add buckwheat, mix well. Add the fresh blood. Mix well over low heat until thick. (About 10 minutes). Pour strained pork stock over the buckwheat. Bring to a boil, simmer 5 minutes.

Rinse casings in warm water. Tie one end and fill loosely with buckwheat mixture. The buckwheat mixture should be of a pouring consistency. Tie ends of the casing. Do not overfill or it will burst.)

Place kyshka (buckwheat sausage) on a rack in a shallow pan of boiling water. Prick with a needle in several places and boil for 25 minutes, uncovered. Remove carefully, cool and store.

To serve brush kyshka with margarine or oil, place in pan with ½ cup water, heat for 25 minutes at 275°F. You may also slice kyshka into 1½" pieces, fry briefly in oil in a frying pan. Serve hot.

See photograph page 34.

Ukrainian Sausage and Sauerkraut

1	ring Ukrainian	1 tbsp.	oil
	sausage	1 qt.	sauerkraut
¼ cup	onions, chopped		

Fry onion in oil until light brown. Mix with sauerkraut and sliced sausage. Place in roaster, and bake for ½ hour in 350°F oven.

See photograph page 50.

Nachinka

1	*medium onion*	1 tsp.	*salt*
¼ lb.	*butter*	1 qt.	*warm milk*
1 cup	*cornmeal*	4	*eggs, well-beaten*
1 tsp.	*sugar*	1 tsp.	*baking powder*

Sauté chopped onion in butter. Do not brown. Turn heat to low. Add cornmeal to butter and mix well. Add the sugar, salt and warm milk. Stir slowly until the cornmeal begins to thicken. Remove from heat. Add the eggs and baking powder. Mix well. Pour into a greased 3-quart casserole. Bake at 325°F for 1 hour.

See photograph page 50.

Holubtsi (Cabbage Rolls) Fillings

Rice and Meat Filling:

½ lb.	*ground beef*	4 tbsp.	*oil*
1	*medium onion, chopped*		

Prepare rice as indicated in cabbage roll recipe page 18. Brown hamburger and onion in oil. Add the browned hamburger to the rice, mix well and then proceed in making the cabbage rolls. See page 18.

Buckwheat Filling:

2 cups	*whole buckwheat, washed well*	1	*medium onion, chopped*
4 cups	*water*	1 tsp.	*salt*
1 tsp.	*salt*	½ tsp.	*pepper*
½ lb.	*fried bacon, crumbled*		

Bring the buckwheat to a boil, turning heat to low until all of the water is absorbed. Add fried bacon and onions. Season with salt and pepper. Stir well. The filling is now ready to place into cabbage leaves and roll into cabbage rolls.

See photographs page 18 and 50.

Polynytsia

6	eggs, well-beaten	2 tsp.	baking powder
1 cup	cold water	4½ cups	flour, approximately
1 tsp.	salt		

Beat eggs, add water. Sift dry ingredients and add to egg mixture. Mix thoroughly and knead. Then roll out to 1½" thickness and pat into a cookie sheet. Prick the dough with a fork in several places. Bake at 350°F for 45 minutes. Cool and slice into small cubes. Set aside.

Nachinka for Polynytsia:

¼ cup	chopped onion		chopped parsley or
¼ cup	chopped celery		dill
¼ cup	butter	1 tsp.	sage
	Polynytsia, cubed	5	eggs, beaten
1 tsp.	salt	2 cups	chicken broth
¼ tsp.	pepper		

Fry onions and celery in butter and pour over cubes of polynytsia to which salt, pepper, sage, and parsley have been added. Add beaten eggs to broth and stir into mixture. Pour into a greased roaster. Bake at 325° for 2 to 2½ hours.

Khrustyky (Sweet Nothings)

6	egg yolks	1 tsp.	sugar
1 cup	flour		pinch of salt
1 tsp.	vinegar		

Beat the egg yolks well, add sugar, vinegar, and flour. Mix well, then knead dough until smooth, on a lightly floured board. Cover with a warm bowl, let stand 10 to 15 minutes.

Roll the dough out paper thin and cut in 1" wide strips, cut the strips about 2" long. Slit each in the centre and pass both ends through, like tieing a bow. Fry in deep fat as you would donuts. Drain and sprinkle with icing sugar.

Nalysnyky (Ukrainian Crêpes)

2	eggs	½ cup	flour, sifted
½ cup	milk	¼ tsp.	salt
3 tbsp.	water		

Double the recipe for 13" x 9" glass pan.

Beat eggs until light and add the remaining ingredients.

Use a small frying pan (6" in diameter). Butter it lightly and heat well. Pour a few tablespoons of the batter into the pan, just enough to give it a thin coating. Tilt the pan back and forth to spread the batter evenly. Cook the cakes over a moderate heat. When lightly browned on the bottom, remove the cakes and stack on a plate. They should not be turned over. This is the secret to tender cakes. In other words, they should just be cooked on one side. Continue baking in this manner until all the batter is used. Butter the pan lightly each time.

Spread the cakes with a sweet or savory filling. When rolling the cakes with filling, place browned side on the outside. Arrange the rolled cakes in a buttered baking dish. Dot each layer with butter. Bake in 350°F oven for 20 minutes. Serve savory cakes with sour cream. A double recipe yields about 26 cakes.

See photograph page 50.

Nalysnyky Fillings

Cottage Cheese (Savory) Filling:

2 cups	cottage cheese	¼ tsp.	salt
2	egg yolks	1 tsp.	chopped dill, if
2 tbsp.	cream (or milk)		desired

Mash the cottage cheese or press through a sieve. Add all the remaining ingredients, mix thoroughly. Spread 1 tbsp. of the filling on the nalysnyky and roll. Proceed as directed in the recipe for nalysnyky. Serve savory nalysnyky with sour cream, if desired.

Crushed Fruit Filling:

Fill nalysnyky with crushed sweetened strawberries, raspberries, blueberries, pitted cherries, or other fruit.

These can be served with whipped cream.

Korzi Z Makom

3 cups	flour	1 tbsp.	oil
1 tsp.	salt	1¼ cups	water

Combine all ingredients.

Knead and roll to about ½″ thickness. Bake on ungreased cookie sheet at 350°F till golden brown, about 8-10 minutes. Cool. Break into small pieces and place in large pot or casserole with lid.

2 cups	poppy seeds	¼ cup	honey or
2-3 cups	hot water	⅓ cup	sugar

Grind poppy seeds.

Add hot water and honey or sugar to taste. Bring this to a boil. Pour this mixture over Korzi, mix well, cover and let stand to soften — 20-30 minutes.

See photograph page 50.

Ukrainian Torte

12	large eggs, separated	1 oz.	semisweet chocolate, grated
1½ cups	sugar		
1 cup	very fine bread crumbs	1 tbsp.	coffee (not instant)
4 cups	ground walnuts	1	orange, juice and rind

Method — Beat yolks, gradually adding sugar until light and lemon colored. Combine with remaining ingredients, except juice, mixture will be quite thick, mix thoroughly. Beat egg whites until stiff. Add orange juice and rind, fold in.

Grease 11" springform pan with lard not butter, and coat with bread crumbs. Bake at 350°F for 1 hour or until toothpick comes out clean. This will make 3 layers. Cut into layers. When done, place on rack — it might sink a little, run knife around the edge to loosen cake, but do not loosen the sides of the spring-form pan for about an hour. Leave on rack until cool.

Variations:

To make an almond layer torte:

6	large eggs, separated	½ cup	fine bread crumbs
1 cup	sugar	½	lemon, juice and rind
1 cup	almonds, finely ground		

Method — Same as above torte. Cut into 2 layers.

Filling: (for 5 layers)

1 lb.	unsalted butter	1½ cups	icing sugar

Beat this thoroughly until very light.

Custard — Bird custard filling:

Cook as directed on box, but add 1 extra tbsp. of powder for a thicker custard. While cooking, add 1 tbsp. butter. Combine with icing sugar mixture. For a variation of custard, coffee may be added or liqueur, chocolate etc.

See photograph page 130.

Yeast-Raised Rohalyky (Crescents)

2 tbsp.	yeast	4 cups	flour
1 tsp.	sugar	4	eggs, beaten
½ cup	warm water	1 tsp.	salt
1 cup	butter		

Dissolve yeast and sugar in ½ cup water. Let stand until softened. Rub butter into flour as for pie crust. Beat eggs and salt together. Add dissolved yeast and mix with flour mixture to make a soft dough. Place dough in plastic bag and tie tightly. Fill bowl with lukewarm water and place plastic bag with dough into water. Let stand until dough rises to the top, about 1 hour. Take a piece of dough about the size of a tennis ball and roll out into a circle on surface which has been sprinkled with sugar, about ¼" thick. Cut into 8 wedges. Place 1 tsp. of desired filling on wide end of wedge and roll up to the point. Place them on a greased baking sheet and let rise 15 minutes. Bake at 375°F for 12 to 15 minutes, or until done.

Rohalyky Filling:

6 oz.	walnuts	¾ cups	sugar
½ cup	oatmeal	1 tsp.	vanilla
3	egg whites, stiffly beaten	½ tsp.	cinnamon

Grind walnuts and oatmeal together in food chopper. Add remaining ingredients and use as filling for rohalyky.

See photograph page 130.

Ukrainian Honey Cookies

3 tbsp.	butter	½ cup	milk
½ cup	white sugar	4 cups	flour
1 cup	honey	3 tsp.	baking soda
2	eggs		

Cream butter, sugar, and honey. Add eggs and beat well. Add milk, sifted flour, and baking soda. Mix. Refrigerate for 1 hour. Drop by teaspoonful on greased cookie sheet and bake in 350°F oven for 15-20 minutes.

Honey Cake

4	eggs, separated	3 tsp.	baking powder
1 cup	white sugar	1 cup	strong coffee,
1 cup	honey, liquified		lukewarm
¾ cup	vegetable oil (corn)	1 cup	nuts, finely chopped
3 cups	flour	⅛ tsp.	salt
1 tsp.	baking soda	¼ tsp.	cinnamon or other
			spice as desired

Cream egg yolks with sugar. Add honey in liquid form, stir as you add oil. Sift all dry ingredients and add to the above. Add coffee as you mix. Mix in nuts and add well-beaten egg whites, salt, and cinnamon. Mix all ingredients lightly.

Bake in 2 loaf pans, lined with wax paper. Bake for 1 hour at 350°F. When top of cake is spongy to touch, it is done.

Kalyna Pyrizhky
(Cranberry Pyrizhky)

3 cups	flour	2	eggs
¼ cup	sugar	1 cup	creamilk
½ tsp.	salt	2 tbsp.	flour
1½ tsp.	baking powder	1 cup	sugar
1 cup	margarine	3 cups	Kalyna (high bush
			cranberries)

Place dry ingredients in bowl, rub in margarine as for pies, beat eggs and creamilk together, add to flour mixture. Knead lightly, chill for 2 hours. Add 2 tbsp. of flour to 1 cup sugar and set aside.

Pinch off small amounts of dough, roll into rounds about 5″ in diameter. Place 2 tbsp. of cranberries in the center, sprinkle with 1 tbsp. of sugar mixture. Pleat dough around filling to form tart with open centre. Place on a cookie sheet, bake at 350°F until golden, about 20-25 minutes. Makes about 2 dozen. These may be eaten either plain or with cream. See photograph page 130.

Breads, Crêpes, and Muffins

Хліби

Air Buns

1 tbsp.	yeast	½ cup	water, lukewarm
1 tbsp.	sugar		

Dissolve yeast and sugar in water, about 10 minutes.

½ cup	sugar	2 tbsp.	vinegar
½ cup	shortening	4 cups	lukewarm water
1 tsp.	salt	8-10 c.	flour

Combine sugar, shortening, salt, vinegar, and water. Add yeast and enough flour so that dough will not stick to hands. Knead 10 minutes. Let rise 2 hours in a warm place. Knead down, let rise 1 hour. Form into small buns. Place on cooking sheet. Let rise 2 hours. Bake in 400°F oven 15-20 minutes.

See photograph page 66.

Crescents

4 cups	flour	1 tbsp.	dry yeast
1 lb.	shortening (Crisco)	1 cup	milk, lukewarm
1 tsp.	salt	2	eggs, well-beaten

Mix flour with shortening and salt. Combine yeast and milk, let stand for 10 minutes. Add eggs, stir into flour mixture. Mix dough well. Keep in covered bowl in refrigerator overnight.

Next morning roll out dough on granulated sugar. Cut in triangles. Place a small amount of filling on wide end, roll up and place on greased cookie sheet. Bake at 350°F for 20-30 minutes until light golden brown.

Filling:

8 oz.	dried apricots	½ cup	water
¼ cup	sugar		

Combine and cook for 20 minutes. You may also use mincemeat or any other desired filling.

Bacon Buns

2 tbsp.	yeast	1 tsp.	sugar
½ cup	water, lukewarm		

Combine until yeast and sugar are dissolved.

2 cups	warm milk	5½-6 c.	flour
3 tbsp.	sugar	1 tbsp.	salt
½ cup	shortening, melted	1	egg, beaten with
	or, oil	1 tbsp.	water
2	eggs, beaten		

Combine milk, sugar, and shortening. Add beaten eggs. Add yeast and enough flour to make a soft dough. Cover, let rise 45 minutes. Pinch off small pieces of dough. Flatten with fingers. Place teaspoonful of filling on dough. Pinch together and shape into crescents on greased cookie sheets. Let rise 15-20 minutes. Bake 20-25 minutes at 375°F. These should be brushed with beaten egg and water before baking.

Filling:

1 lb.	side bacon	1	medium onion,
1 lb.	back bacon		finely chopped
¼ tsp.	pepper or to taste		

Grind bacon, mix in pepper and onion.

Basic Sweet Dough —
Cinnamon Rolls or Buns

| 2 tsp. | sugar | ½ cup | water, lukewarm |
| 3 tsp. | yeast | | |

Combine until yeast and sugar are dissolved.

5	eggs, well-beaten	10-10½ cups	flour to make a
1 cup	sugar		soft dough
1 cup	vegetable oil	½ cup	margarine or butter
3 cups	lukewarm water		softened
1 tsp.	salt	¾ cup	brown sugar
2 tbsp.	baking powder	1½ tsp.	cinnamon

Beat the eggs well, add sugar in small amounts, then add the oil. Beat well. Add water and some flour with the yeast, beat till smooth. Add more flour to make a soft dough. Let rise twice, punching down when the dough is double in size.

Roll out ½" thick in a rectangular shape. Spread the rolled dough with soft margarine or butter. Sprinkle brown sugar and dust with cinnamon. Roll like a jelly roll, cut slices across 1" wide and place slices in greased pans 1" apart.

Let rise to double in size, brush with melted margarine and bake at 375°F for 20 to 30 minutes.

Cottage Cheese Buns

2 tbsp.	yeast	1 cup	lukewarm water
2 tbsp.	sugar		

Dissolve yeast and sugar in 1 cup of lukewarm water. Let rise 10 minutes.

3	eggs	½ cup	sugar
1 cup	water	1 tsp.	salt
6 tbsp.	oil	6-7 cups	flour, approx.

Beat eggs, add water, oil, and sugar and salt. Add yeast mixture. Add enough flour to make a soft dough. Cover, let rise, knead dough and let rise again. Pinch off small pieces of dough. Flatten with fingers. Place teaspoonful of filling on dough. Pinch together and shape into crescents on greased cookie sheets. Let rise for about 20 minutes. Bake at 325°F for 15 minutes. Brush with butter.

Filling:

1 lb.	cottage cheese	½ cup	dill, chopped
1	egg		salt and pepper
	green onions, as desired		

To serve, pour dill sauce over buns.

Dill Sauce:

1	small onion, chopped	2 tbsp.	butter
¼ cup	dill, chopped	2 cups	whipping cream

Sauté onions and dill in butter. Add whipping cream, simmer for 15 minutes.

Warm 3 dozen buns and pour sauce over buns.

Milk Buns

2 tbsp.	Fleischmann's yeast	⅔ cup	sugar
2 cups	milk, scalded and cooled to lukewarm	½ cup	butter
		1 tsp.	salt
		2	eggs, well-beaten
2 tbsp.	sugar	4½ cups	flour
3 cups	flour		

Dissolve yeast and sugar in milk. Add flour to yeast mixture. Mix and knead until smooth. Put in warm place to rise until doubled — about 1 hour.

Then add remaining ingredients. Mix and let rise about 1½ hours. Roll and cut in any shape desired. Place in greased pans. Bake at 350°F for 20-25 minutes.

Overnight Buns

1 tbsp.	yeast dissolved in ½ cup lukewarm water	½ cup	sugar
		½ cup	margarine
		1	egg, beaten
3½-4 c.	flour	1 cup	cold milk
½ tsp.	salt		

Mix flour, salt, and sugar, cut in margarine as for pie crust. Add egg, yeast, and milk. Mix as for dough. Work well. Knead 10 minutes. Put in in cool place overnight. In morning, roll out and shape into buns, (cinnamon, plain, etc.). Let rise 1½ hours. Bake at 325°F-350°F for 20-25 minutes.

Two-Hour Buns

2 tbsp.	instant yeast	8 tbsp.	sugar or honey
	(Fermipan)	6 tbsp.	oil
7-8 cups	flour	1 tsp.	salt
2	eggs	3 cups	water

Mix yeast in 4 cups of flour. In separate large bowl whip eggs, sugar, oil, salt and water. Add flour-yeast mixture. Blend well and add remaining flour. Let rise for 15 minutes. Punch down. Let rise for 15 minutes. Punch down and form into buns. Place in greased pan and let rise for 1 hour.

Bake at 350°F for 15-18 minutes.

Makes 4-5 dozen. ⅃.

Note: if using whole wheat flour add ⅓-½ cup of gluten to the flour for lighter buns.

Never-Fail Buns

| 3 cups | warm water | 2 tbsp. | yeast |
| 1½ tsp. | salt | ½ cup | sugar (less for bread) |

Dissolve yeast, sugar and salt in water for 10 minutes.

| 4 | eggs, beaten | 10 cups | flour or less |
| ½ cup | oil | | |

Combine eggs and oil, stir in yeast mixture, add flour. Blend well, cover, and let rise 2 hours. Do not punch. Make into buns or bread. Let rise 1½ hours. Bake buns, 25 minutes at 375°F. Bake bread, 15 minutes at 400°F, then 25 minutes at 375°F.

Babka (Easter Bread)

A good babka is rich, tender, fine-textured and very light. It is baked in tall round pans, such as 2 or 3 lb. coffee cans and is always sliced in rounds across the loaf.

2 tbsp.	dry yeast	1 tsp.	sugar
⅓ cup	lukewarm water		

Combine until yeast and sugar are dissolved.

1 cup	milk		rind 1 lemon, grated
½ cup	butter		
8	egg yolks and 2 egg whites	1 tsp.	vanilla
		1 tsp.	salt
1 cup	sugar	6 cups	flour
½ cup	orange juice rind of 1 orange, grated	½ cup	raisins

Boil milk, add butter and cool.

Beat egg yolks and whites till light. Add sugar and beat again. Then add eggs to milk mixture. Add orange juice and rinds, vanilla and salt and add yeast which has risen.

Mix with spoon and add flour and raisins (which have been washed, dried and mixed with a little flour) add and knead and let rise. Knead again and let rise till double in size. Form dough into a ball, small enough to fill ⅓ of a container. Let rise in warm place. Bake in preheated oven at 350°F for 30 minutes.

See photographs pages 34 and 66.

Breads

1. Air Buns (p. 60)
2. Basic Sweet Dough — Cinnamon Rolls or Buns (p. 62)
3. Kolach Recipe — Braided Breads (p. 12)
4. Paska (p. 30)
5. Babka (p. 32/33/66)
6. Easter Doves (p. 13/31)
7. Five-Grain Health Bread (p. 67)
8. Pampushky (p. 22)
9. Potato Bread (p. 68)

Five-Grain Health Bread

1 tbsp.	granular yeast	½ cup	quick cooking rolled oats
3 cups	lukewarm water		
½ cup	honey	½ cup	cornmeal
⅓ cup	shortening (room temperature)	5 cups	unsifted all purpose flour (divided)
1½ cups	whole wheat flour	1 tbsp.	salt
1½ cups	dark rye flour	¾ cup	skim milk powder

In a very large bowl soak yeast, honey, and shortening in the lukewarm water for 10 or 15 minutes. In the meantime, measure all remaining ingredients and add, except 3 cups of the white flour, in order given, stir 50 times. Cover and let rise in warm place until double in bulk (about 2 hours). This dough is moist and sticky.

Sprinkle kneading board with all of the remaining white flour Punch down, turn out dough on board and knead flour into it to make the dough firm enough to handle. Now knead it 250 times.

Shape into a 2' roll. Cut in half and shape into 2 loaves and place in 2 standard buttered loaf pans and let rise. Bake at 400°F for 20 minutes. Then reduce heat to 350°F and bake 40 minutes longer.

See photograph page 66.

Onion Cheese Bread

3 cups	flour	4	green onions, finely chopped or ½ cup white onions, finely chopped
1 tbsp.	baking powder		
1½ tsp.	salt		
3 tbsp.	sugar		
1 cup	sharp Cheddar cheese, grated	1	bottle beer

Combine first 6 ingredients. Mix in beer. Pour into greased loaf pan. Bake at 350°F for 1½ hours.

Potato Bread

This is a delicious fine-textured bread with a crisp crust.

2 tsp.	sugar	2 tbsp.	sugar
¾ cup	warm water	2 tsp.	salt
2 tbsp.	dry yeast	1¼ cups	milk
6 cups	all purpose flour	1½ cups	potatoes, mashed
	(approx.) or whole-	¼ cup	margarine or butter
	wheat flour	2	eggs

Stir 2 teaspoons of sugar with the water until dissolved. Sprinkle yeast over, and let stand 10 minutes. Stir well.

Combine 1½ cups of the flour, sugar and salt in a large bowl. Heat next 3 ingredients in a saucepan, until margarine is melted, cool until just warm. Add to the flour mixture, beat until smooth.

Beat in yeast mixture and eggs, then 1 cup of the flour. (Mixture should be like thick batter.) Beat at low speed 2 minutes. With a wooden spoon, stir in about 3 cups of the flour, or enough to make a soft dough.

Turn dough on a floured board and knead until smooth and elastic, about 10 minutes, kneading in about ½ cup of flour, or enough to make it still soft but easy to handle.

Put dough in a large, greased bowl and turn it over so the top of the dough is greased. Cover with a damp cloth and let rise in a warm place until double, about 1½ hours. Punch dough down, turn out on a board and knead lightly. Cover with a damp cloth and let rest 15 minutes.

Grease 2 — 9" x 5" x 3" pans. Shape dough into 2 loaves and put in pans. Cover with a damp cloth and let rise until double, about 1 hour. Heat oven to 400°F. Bake loaves until they sound hollow when tapped on top, about 40 minutes. Cool on racks.

Makes 2 loaves.

Variation: Add onion, fried in oil, to the mashed potatoes and continue.

See photograph page 66.

Hobo Bread

1½ cups	boiling water	2 tsp.	vanilla
3¾ cups	raisins	¾ tsp.	salt
4 tsp.	baking soda	4 cups	flour or 3 scant
¼ cup	margarine		cups white flour
1 cup	brown sugar		and 1 cup whole
¼ cup	white sugar		wheat flour
¼ cup	molasses	2	large eggs

Boil raisins and water together, cool slightly and stir in remaining ingredients. Mix well.

Fill tins (small juice cans or other desired sizes) only half full. Bake at 350°F for 1 hour.

Freezes well.

Boiled Raisin Muffins

1½ cups	raisins, washed	1 tsp.	soda
¾ cup	brown sugar	¾ cup	sour cream
½ cup	Crisco shortening	1½ cup	flour
1	large egg, beaten	1 tsp.	salt
1 tsp.	vanilla	1 tsp.	baking powder
1 tsp.	lemon peel, grated	½ cup	chopped walnuts

Simmer raisins in barely enough water to cover, about 10 minutes. Some water should remain.

Beat sugar and shortening till creamy. Add the beaten egg, vanilla and peel. Put the soda into the sour cream. Sift flour and salt with the baking powder. Add the flour and sour cream alternately to the egg mixture. Add raisins and chopped nuts. Mix together. Fill 24 lined muffin cups. Bake at 350°F for 25 minutes.

Banana Muffins

½ cup	butter or margarine	1 cup	banana, mashed
1 cup	sugar	1½ cups	flour
1	egg	1 tsp.	baking powder
2 tbsp.	milk	1 tsp.	vanilla
1 tsp.	baking soda		

Cream butter and sugar. Add egg and milk. Add soda to banana, add to egg and sugar mixture and beat again. Add sifted flour, baking powder, and vanilla. Use paper cupcake liners in muffin tins. Fill ⅔ full with muffin mixture. Bake for 20 minutes at 350°F.

Makes 24 medium muffins.

Favourite Moist Bran Muffins

3 cups	buttermilk	3 cups	100% bran cereal

Mix the above and let stand.

1 cup	oil	3 tsp.	baking soda
1 cup	brown sugar	2 tsp.	salt
1 cup	white sugar	3 cups	flour
3	eggs	3 tsp.	baking powder
1 tsp.	vanilla	1 cup	raisins, washed

Mix oil, brown sugar, white sugar, and eggs. Add vanilla, soda, and salt and beat. Stir in buttermilk and bran mixture. Sift flour and baking powder and add to the above along with the raisins. Mix well, quickly — just until well blended.

Bake in greased and floured muffin tins for 20 minutes at 350°F.

These freeze very well.

Bran Muffins

2	eggs	1 tsp.	salt
1 cup	sugar	2 tsp.	baking powder
¾ cup	oil	2 cups	flour
2 cups	milk	1½ cups	raisins or
1 cup	bran		blueberries or
1 tsp.	vanilla		grated apple
1 tsp.	baking soda		with cinnamon

Cream eggs and sugar, add oil and beat. Add milk, bran, and vanilla, mix well. Add dry ingredients and fruit, mix lightly. Let rest 5 minutes. Fill muffin tins ⅔ full. Bake at 350°F for 20-25 minutes. Makes 24 muffins.

Apple-Cheese Muffins

½ cup	margarine	¾ cup	rolled oats
½ cup	sugar	1 cup	apple pie filling
2	eggs	⅔ cup	sharp cheese, grated
1 tsp.	baking soda	½ cup	nuts
½ tsp.	salt	¼ cup	milk
1½ cups	flour		

Cream margarine and sugar, add eggs. Combine dry ingredients, add to sugar mixture with pie filling, (apple pieces may be cut up if too large) cheese, and nuts. Stir in milk last. Fill muffin pans ⅔ full. Bake at 400°F, 20 to 25 minutes. Makes 24 medium muffins.

Pumpkin Muffins

4	eggs	1 tbsp.	cinnamon
2 cups	sugar	2 tsp.	baking soda
1½ cups	cooking oil	2 tsp.	baking powder
14 oz.	can pumpkin	1 tsp.	salt
3 cups	flour	2 cups	chocolate chips

Beat eggs slightly. Add sugar, oil, and pumpkin. Beat thoroughly. Sift dry ingredients over creamed mixture. Blend well. Stir in chocolate chips. Put mixture in muffin pans. Bake 25 minutes at 350°F. Makes 3 dozen.

Crêpe Batter

1 cup	all-purpose flour	¼ tsp.	salt
2	eggs	2 tbsp.	melted butter or
½ cup	milk		margarine
½ cup	water		

Place all ingredients in bowl and beat until smooth. Let stand for 1 or 2 hours. Grease non-stick pan with butter and place 2 tablespoons batter on pan. Tilt pan so that batter covers the pan. These should be very thin. Brown 1 side only. Makes 16 crêpes.

Cottage Cheese Filling for Crêpes

1½ cups	cottage cheese (put through a sieve so it is very fine)	1	egg
		½ cup	sugar
		¼ cup	butter, melted

Combine all ingredients, except for butter. Mix well. Spread heaping tablespoonful on each crêpe. Roll up. Place in buttered casserole. Drizzle ¼ cup melted butter over crêpes. Bake 30 minutes at 325°F. Nice for brunch.

Fruit Filling for Crêpes

| 3 oz. | Philadelphia cream cheese | ¼ cup | brown sugar |
| ⅓ cup | sour cream | | pie filling — apple, cherry or peach |

Combine cheese, sour cream and sugar. Beat until smooth and creamy. Spread 1 tablespoon over crêpe. Then use 1 heaping tablespoon pie filling on each crêpe. Roll up. Place in buttered casserole. Bake 15-20 minutes at 325°F (or 3 minutes in microwave). Serve with small scoop of ice cream on each serving. Garnish with nuts.

Crêpes Marquis

Crêpe Batter:

3	eggs, beaten	½ tsp.	salt
⅔ cup	flour	1 cup	milk

Combine eggs, flour, salt, and milk, beat until smooth. Let stand for 30 minutes. For each crêpe, pour ¼ cup batter into hot, lightly greased skillet. Cook on 1 side only.

Filling:

8	slices bacon	10 oz.	mushrooms, drained, sliced
½ cup	onions, finely chopped	2 cups	shredded Cheddar cheese
½ cup	green peppers, chopped	8 oz.	tomato sauce

Fry bacon until crisp, drain, reserving 2 tablespoons fat. Sauté onions and green peppers in bacon fat until tender. Chop bacon. Add bacon, mushrooms and 1½ cups cheese to the onion mixture. Mix lightly. Fill each crêpe with about ¼ cup mixture; roll up.

Place crêpes in baking pan. Top with tomato sauce. Bake at 350°F for 15 minutes. Sprinkle with remaining cheese, continue baking until cheese melts.

Serves: 6.

Mushroom Crêpes with Cream Sauce

Crêpe Batter:

2	eggs		¼ tsp.	salt
1¼ cups	milk		2 tbsp.	melted butter or
1 cup	flour			vegetable oil

Beat together the eggs and milk. Sift the flour with the salt and add to the egg and milk mixture. Add the melted butter or vegetable oil and blend thoroughly. Allow the mixture to stand for at least an hour before using. (If the batter is too thick, add a little milk and mix.)

Pour 1 or 2 tablespoons of the batter in the centre of a hot, lightly-oiled frying pan. Tilt to spread the batter to the edges of the pan. Cook until the top is dry. Turn over and cook the other side for about 15 seconds. Makes 12 large or 24 small.

Sauce: **Filling:**

½ cup	butter		4 cups	sliced mushrooms
½ cup	flour		¾ cup	butter
1 tsp.	salt		½ tsp.	salt
¼ tsp.	pepper		¼ tsp.	pepper
4 cups	cream			
⅔ cup	grated cheese			

For the cheese sauce, melt butter in a saucepan. Remove from heat, stir in flour, salt, and pepper until smooth. Return to low heat, cook for 5 minutes. Slowly pour in the cream, stirring constantly. Cook until thickened. Do not boil. Add cheese, stir until cheese has melted and sauce is smooth and creamy.

For the filling, sauté the mushrooms in half the butter for about 5 minutes. Pour in half the cheese sauce and salt and pepper to taste. Mix well.

Fill each crêpe with the mushroom filling. Fold over and place in a buttered shallow baking dish. Dot with the remaining butter and pour on the rest of the sauce. Bake in a 350°F oven for ½ hour. Serves: 6.

Plain Pancakes

2 cups	flour	2	eggs, well-beaten
4 tsp.	baking powder	2 tbsp.	butter or lard,
½ tsp.	salt		melted
2½ cups	milk		

Preheat griddle to 400°F. Mix dry ingredients. Add milk to beaten eggs. Mix the liquids with the flour mixture and blend. Add melted butter or lard. Pour ¼ cup of batter on hot lightly-greased griddle. Fry until golden brown, turn once.

Oatmeal Pancakes

1½ cups	rolled oats	½ cup	whole-wheat flour
2 cups	milk	½ cup	all-purpose flour
1 tbsp.	baking powder	1 tbsp.	brown sugar
1 tsp.	salt	2	eggs, beaten
½ tsp.	cinnamon	¼ cup	butter, melted

Blend rolled oats and milk, let stand for 5 minutes. Stir together dry ingredients. Add dry ingredients, eggs, and melted butter to oats. Pour ¼ cup of batter on hot, lightly-greased griddle. Fry until golden brown. Turn once.

Makes about 16-18 medium-size pancakes.

Yogurt Pancakes

1	egg	1 cup	flour
1 cup	plain yogurt	2 tbsp.	sugar
	(at room	½ tsp.	baking soda
	temperature)	¼ tsp.	salt
1 tbsp.	vegetable oil	1 tsp.	baking powder

Beat egg until thick, add yogurt, beating constantly. Drizzle oil into yogurt mixture. Beat well. Add dry ingredients and mix. Fry on hot, greased griddle until golden brown. Turn once. Serve with butter and syrup.

Drop Doughnuts

2 tsp.	baking soda	1 tsp.	salt
4 tsp.	cream of tartar	1 tsp.	nutmeg
2 cups	milk	2 tsp.	lemon extract
4	eggs	1 tsp.	ginger
1 cup	white sugar	4 cups	flour
1 cup	brown sugar	1 tsp.	baking powder
3 tbsp.	oil		

Dissolve soda and cream of tartar in milk. Beat together eggs, sugar, and oil. Add milk, salt, nutmeg, lemon extract, ginger. Add enough flour to make dough easy to handle, add baking powder. This makes about 100, walnut-sized, drop doughnuts. You can also roll and cut with doughnut cutter. Drop with teaspoon into hot fat or oil at 375°F for about 3 minutes. Dust with icing sugar, or at Christmas time ice with chocolate icing then dip in chopped walnuts or ice with white icing, dip in coconut and call them Yule Nuts or Snow Balls.

Spudnuts

2 tbsp.	yeast	1 cup	warm water
2 tsp.	sugar		

Dissolve yeast and sugar in water, about 10 minutes.

5	eggs	1 cup	butter or margarine, melted
1 cup	sugar		
2 cups	mashed potatoes	1½ tsp.	salt
4 cups	milk	2 tsp.	nutmeg
9 cups	flour (approx.) to make a soft dough		

Beat eggs and sugar, add mashed potatoes. Add milk, melted butter, salt, and nutmeg. Add the dissolved yeast. Add enough flour to make a soft dough. Let rise once, then roll out and cut with doughnut cutter, let rise, then fry on both sides in deep fat. You can use 2 cups water and 2 cups evaporated milk instead of the whole milk.

Yield: 90 spudnuts.

Salads, Soups
and Vegetables

Салати, Супи
і Ярина

Marinated Carrots

2 lbs.	carrots, unpeeled	10 oz.	can tomato soup
1	large Spanish onion, thinly sliced	1 cup	white sugar
		½ cup	salad oil
1	large green pepper, thinly sliced in rings	¾ cup	vinegar
		1 tsp.	salt
		½ tsp.	pepper
2	stalks of celery, diced		

Wash and cook unpeeled carrots until tender-crisp, don't overcook. Drain. Put in cold water and peel. (Cooking carrots this way gives them a bright color). Cut in half lengthwise in about 2″ strips, if large carrots. Add onion rings, pepper, and celery.

Combine remaining ingredients in a saucepan. Bring to a boil, stirring to dissolve sugar. Pour over vegetables and cook on low heat for 5 minutes. If desired, pack in hot sterilized jars and seal. Cool and store. Allow to marinate at least overnight before using.

This makes 4 pints.

Marge's Coleslaw

7	heads of cabbage, shredded	12	green onions, cut up
6	carrots, grated	4	green peppers, chopped

Mix all vegetables together.

Dressing:

3 cups	sugar	6 tsp.	salt
3 cups	Crisco oil (do not substitute)	4 cups	vinegar

Mix together and just bring to a boil. Pour over cabbage and other vegetables. Let stand 12 hours. Drain well before serving.

Serves 100 people.

Creamy Beet Salad with Dill

5	medium fresh beets, remove tops and stems	½ cup	whipping cream
		¼ tsp.	salt
		⅛ tsp.	pepper
⅛ tsp.	salt	1 tsp.	lemon juice
1 tbsp.	butter	2 tbsp.	chopped dill
		1-2 tbsp.	sour cream

Place beets in a large saucepan and add enough cold water to cover. Add salt and bring to boil. Cover and simmer for 45 minutes to 1 hour or until tender.

Drain and cool. Peel and cut into small cubes. Melt butter in frying pan, add cubed beets. Sauté 2 minutes, stirring well. Pour in whipping cream and cook over medium heat about 5 minutes or until cream is thickened. Season with salt, pepper, and lemon juice.

Remove from heat and stir in chopped dill and sour cream. Mix well.

Chill or serve at room temperature.

Sweet and Sour Coleslaw

3 lbs.	cabbage, shredded	2 cups	sugar
1	large onion, finely chopped	1 cup	vinegar
		¾ cup	oil
1	green pepper, finely chopped	1 tbsp.	salt
		1 tbsp.	celery seed

Shred the cabbage, onion, and green pepper and combine. Over this sprinkle the sugar and let stand while you prepare the dressing. Bring the vinegar, oil, salt, and celery seed to the boiling point. Pour over the vegetables. Combine thoroughly. Put in refrigerator to chill. Will keep for at least a week. Drain before serving.

Caesar Salad

1	clove garlic, chopped	½ cup	salad oil
¼ cup	salad oil	1 tsp.	Worcestershire sauce
2½ cups	bread cubes		pepper
8 cups	salad greens,		salt
	preferably	1	egg
	Romaine lettuce	½ cup	lemon juice
⅓ cup	Parmesan cheese		

Early in Day:

Quarter garlic, drop into ¼ cup salad oil, set aside. Toast bread cubes in pan at 320°F. Tear lettuce into bite-size pieces in salad bowl. Refrigerate all.

Just Before Serving:

Sprinkle greens with cheese, drizzle on ½ cup salad oil mixed with Worcestershire sauce, salt and pepper. Toss gently until every leaf glistens. Break whole raw egg onto greens, pour lemon juice over all, toss until egg specks disappear. Now pour the ¼ cup oil you set aside over bread squares, toss, sprinkle over greens. Toss salad, serve at once.

Note: Ingredients for dressing can also be mixed in blender and then poured over greens.

Sauerkraut Salad

½ cup	oil	1 cup	green pepper, chopped
½ cup	vinegar		chopped
1 cup	sugar	½ cup	red pepper, chopped
32 oz.	jar sauerkraut	1 cup	carrots, shredded
1 cup	onion, chopped	1 cup	celery, diced

Combine oil, vinegar, and sugar. Bring to a boil. Cool. Mix sauerkraut with remaining ingredients. Pour oil mixture over all. Refrigerate 24 hours. This is perfect with barbecued roast beef.

Ginger Ale Fruit Mold

1 cup	hot water	1 cup	fruit cocktail,
3 oz.	pkg. lemon-flavoured		drained
	gelatin		juice of ½ lemon
¾ cup	ginger ale		

Filling:

1 cup	cottage cheese	1 tbsp.	cream
¼ cup	pecans	1 tbsp.	mayonnaise
4	maraschino cherries, sliced		

Stir hot water into gelatin until dissolved. Chill until cool but not thickened. Stir ginger ale, fruit cocktail, and lemon juice into cooled gelatin. Pour into ring mold rinsed in cold water. Chill until firm. At serving time, combine cottage cheese, pecans, cherries, cream, and mayonnaise. Unmold fruit gelatin ring, fill center with cottage cheese mixture.

Coleslaw Oil Dressing

⅓ cup	white sugar	1 tsp.	salt
½ cup	white vinegar		garlic salt, to
⅓ cup	oil		taste

Bring the first 4 ingredients to a full boil. Cool and add garlic salt to taste.

Anna's Salad Dressing

¾ cup	sugar	3	eggs, well-beaten
2 tbsp.	flour	1 cup	vinegar
1 tsp.	mustard	2 cups	boiling water
¼ tsp.	salt		

Combine all ingredients in a heavy stainless steel or enamel pan. Cook until thick. This is a good basic salad dressing.

Cream of Onion Soup

3 tbsp.	butter, melted	2	chicken-flavored
3 cups	onions, diced		bouillon cubes
¼ tsp.	salt	1 cup	milk
4 cups	water, boiling	⅛ tsp.	pepper
1	medium potato,		
	peeled and diced		

Melt butter in saucepan, add onions, and salt. Fry for 5 minutes. Add potato, 1 cup water, cook over low heat 15 minutes, stir occasionally. Dissolve bouillon cubes in boiling water, add to vegetable mixture, simmer, covered for 20 minutes. Add milk and pepper. Yield 6 servings.

Carrot Soup

6	large carrots	10 oz.	can, cream of
10 oz.	milk		mushroom soup
¼ tsp.	salt		or
⅛ tsp.	pepper	10 oz.	can cream of
			celery soup

Boil carrots and mash. Save the liquid and add enough water to make 2 cups. Add to mashed carrots. Add soup, then stir in milk, salt and pepper. Simmer for a few minutes.

Corn Chowder

¾ cup	celery, diced	14 oz.	can cream corn
¾ cup	onion, chopped	12 oz.	can kernel corn
¼ cup	butter	½ tsp.	basil
1¾ cup	milk	½ tsp.	salt
2-10 oz.	cans cream of		bacon bits (garnish)
	chicken soup		

Sauté celery and onion in butter until tender. Add milk, soup, corn, and seasonings. Heat, stirring occasionally, until chowder is hot but not boiling. Sprinkle bacon bits or pieces on top of chowder for additional flavor.

Tomato Noodle Soup

Noodles:

1	egg	¼ tsp.	salt
¾ cup	flour		

Combine ingredients. Knead well. Roll out thinly and cut into noodles.

¼ cup	celery, diced	10 oz.	condensed tomato
2 tbsp.	onion, chopped		soup
½ cup	carrot, diced	20 oz.	water
½ cup	whipping cream	2 tbsp.	butter
3 tsp.	"Chicken-in-a-Mug"		

Cook vegetables in water until tender. Drain, reserving liquid. Pour whipping cream over vegetables to cover. Boil until slightly thick. Combine tomato soup and water. Add noodles and cook until tender. Add vegetable mixture, reserved liquid, butter, and "Chicken-in-a-Mug".

Fresh Mushroom Soup

2½ lbs.	fresh mushrooms	1-1⅓ c.	flour (or more for
	salt to taste		desired thickness)
5	cloves garlic (or	½ cup	oil
	more according to		
	taste, crushed		

Wash mushrooms well to remove all grit and dirt. Cut in small pieces put into soup pot. Add water to cover mushrooms. (If more water is needed, add after mushrooms are cooked.) Add salt and garlic. Cook for about 1 hour.

Brown flour in oil over medium heat, stirring constantly so that the flour does not burn. Carefully add the browned flour roux to the boiling mushrooms, a little at a time, stir vigorously to prevent lumping. Stir well, simmer until well blended. More roux may be added if a thicker consistency is desired.

Pea Soup

4 tbsp.	margarine	4 cups	water
4 tbsp.	flour	4	carrots, chopped
1	small onion, chopped	1 tsp.	salt
2 tsp.	parsley	¼ tsp.	pepper
4 cups	peas, frozen	½ tsp.	paprika

Cook margarine and flour for a few minutes, until well blended, stir continually. Add onion, stir and cook for a few more minutes, until transparent but not browned. Add remaining ingredients, bring to a boil, simmer for ½ hour. Add noodles (see recipe below).

Noodles:

1½ cup	flour	½ tsp.	salt
1	egg	½ cup	water

Mix all ingredients into a ball, break off little pieces and drop them into the soup. Cook for 15 minutes.

Creamed Spring Borsch (Beet Soup)

6-8	young beets, stalk and leaves	¼ cup	dill greens, chopped few garlic leaves, chopped
5 cups	water		
1	medium onion	2 tsp.	salt
½ cup	broad beans or fresh beans	2 tbsp.	lemon juice or vinegar
½ cup	peas, fresh	3 tbsp.	flour
½ cup	potatoes, diced	½ cup	water
		1 cup	cream or milk

Wash beets thoroughly but do not peel. Rinse leaves and stalks. Set leaves aside, dice beets and stalks. In a large pot add water all of the vegetables, salt, and lemon juice. Add diced leaves last. Do not overcook vegetables. When vegetables are almost done, mix flour in water. Pour into soup, cook for 5 minutes. Add cream or milk and serve. 6-8 servings.

Kapusta

1 lb.	kidney beans	1 cup	peas, frozen or
1 qt.	ham stock		fresh
1 qt.	sauerkraut	1 tsp.	salt
	(rinse with hot	¼ tsp.	pepper
	water in sieve)	1	medium onion
⅓ cup	celery, chopped	1 tbsp.	dill, fresh or
10 oz.	mushrooms, canned,		dried
	stems and pieces	3-4 tbsp.	butter
	if you wish	2 tbsp.	flour

Soak beans overnight in cold water. Wash them well in morning, cover with cold water and bring to boil. Remove foam or rinse off then cover again with cold water. Bring to boil and simmer for 2-3 hours until soft to mash well. Add water if needed to keep from burning.

Put stock and sauerkraut in large pot, bring to boil, simmer for ¾ hour. Add mashed beans, bring to boil, simmer for ½ hour. Add celery, mushrooms, dill, peas, salt, and pepper. Simmer 20 minutes. Brown chopped onion in butter. Add flour, brown lightly, add to broth. Return to boil, simmer for ½ hour. Ready to serve or freeze.

See photograph page 18.

Potato Soup

2 tbsp.	margarine	½ cup	milk
1	medium onion, diced	1 tbsp.	flour
2	potatoes, pared and	1 cup	sour cream
	diced	½ tsp.	salt
1	stalk celery, chopped	¼ tsp.	pepper
1 cup	cabbage, chopped		fresh or dry dillweed
4 cups	chicken stock		

In saucepan melt margarine and sauté onion. Add potatoes, celery, cabbage, and chicken stock. Simmer 15 minutes, until vegetables are tender. Remove 2 cups of cooked vegetables, combine with milk, flour, and sour cream, purée in blender. Stir mixture into soup and reheat. Add salt and pepper to taste. Garnish with dill and serve.

Bean or Carrot Casserole

4 cups	green or yellow wax beans cut in 1" pieces or 4 cups carrots, diced	2 tbsp.	flour
		¼ tsp.	pepper
		1	onion, finely chopped
		1	celery stalk, diced
2 tbsp.	butter	1 cup	sour cream or buttermilk
1 tsp.	salt		
1 tsp.	sugar		

Topping:

2 tbsp.	melted butter	½ lb.	Cheddar cheese, grated
¾ cup	dry breadcrumbs or cornflakes		

Cook the beans, or carrots, in salted water until almost done. Melt the butter and stir in the salt, sugar, flour, pepper, celery and onion. Add the sour cream or buttermilk and mix well, then heat through. Fold in the drained vegetables and put all in a buttered casserole.

For the topping, mix the crumbs with the melted butter, then with the cheese. Sprinkle over the top of the beans or carrots. Bake in a 400°F oven for 20 minutes. A good luncheon or buffet supper dish.

About 6 servings.

Broccoli Dish

10 oz.	pkg. frozen broccoli cooked	½-¾ c.	Cheese Whiz
		10 oz.	can cream of mushroom soup
1 cup	cooked rice		
10 oz.	can water chestnuts, drained and sliced	½ cup	bread crumbs
		1½ tbsp.	melted butter

Mix together and place in a casserole dish. Sprinkle top with bread crumbs which have been sautéed in melted butter. Bake at 350°F for 30 minutes.

Broccoli Casserole

1½ lb.	fresh broccoli, cut up	1 tbsp.	pimiento, chopped
10 oz.	can cream of mushroom soup	1½ tsp.	lemon juice
¼ cup	salad dressing	¼ cup	crushed corn flakes or bread crumbs (optional)
¼ cup	sharp processed cheese, shredded		

Cook broccoli in small amount of salted water until cooked but still crisp. Drain. Put in greased 1½ quart casserole. Combine soup, salad dressing, cheese, pimiento, and lemon juice. Pour over broccoli. Top with crushed corn flakes or fine bread crumbs, if desired. Bake 35 minutes at 350°F.

Curried Baked Cauliflower

1	large head cauliflower	⅓ cup	mayonnaise
½ tsp.	salt	1 tsp.	curry powder
10 oz.	can condensed cream of chicken soup	¾ cup	dried bread crumbs
4 oz.	pkg. Cheddar cheese, shredded (1 cup)	2 tbsp.	butter or margarine, melted

Preheat oven to 350°F. Break cauliflower into flowerets. In large covered saucepan over medium-low heat, cook cauliflower in 1" boiling water with salt for 10 minutes, drain well.

In 2-quart casserole, stir together undiluted soup, cheese, mayonnaise, and curry powder. Add cauliflower, mix well. Toss bread crumbs in melted butter, sprinkle on top.

Bake 30 minutes or until casserole is hot and bubbly. Makes 8-10 servings.

Home-Baked Beans

1 lb.	dried white beans	1 tsp.	salt, or less
2	large onions	1 tsp.	pepper
½ lb.	slab bacon or	½-1 tsp.	dry mustard
	sliced bacon	3 cups	boiling water
¼ cup	molasses		tomato juice
¼ cup	maple syrup		(optional)
½ cup	ketchup		

Place beans in a saucepan, cover with cold water and simmer, uncovered, for 1 hour. Drain and place in large Dutch oven. Peel and chop onions. Remove rind from bacon and chop bacon into pieces. Combine molasses, maple syrup, ketchup, salt, pepper, mustard, and boiling water and pour over beans.

Cover mixture and bake in 250°F oven for 7 to 8 hours. Add a little tomato juice as required, if necessary, to prevent mixture from becoming too dry.

Note: The water the beans were boiled in, can be diluted with tomato juice, to add to beans, when required, to prevent them from getting too dry.

Turnip Casserole

2	medium turnips,	1½ tsp.	salt
	boiled and mashed	¼ tsp.	pepper
1 cup	applesauce	2	eggs
6 tbsp.	butter	¾ cup	bread crumbs
4 tsp.	sugar	1½ tbsp.	butter

Mix first 7 ingredients together and place in uncovered casserole. Sauté bread crumbs in butter and spread on top of turnip.

Bake at 350°F for ½ hour.

Oven-Baked French Fries

| 2 | medium potatoes | salt to taste |
| 1 tbsp. | pure vegetable oil | |

Chill the potatoes, then peel them and cut into French-fry sticks. Preheat oven to 450°F. Pour the oil into the center of a large baking sheet. Add the cut potatoes, and mix by hand until coated. Spread the potatoes out evenly over the baking sheet and salt them. Bake for 35 to 40 minutes or until golden brown, watch carefully. Turn once. Serves 2.

Potato Surprise Bake

2 lbs.	frozen hash browns, slightly thawed	8 oz.	sour cream
		½ pt	whipping cream
10 oz.	can cream of potato soup	1	medium onion, diced
		¾ cup	nippy cheese, grated
		2 tbsp.	butter
10 oz.	can cream of celery soup	¼ cup	corn flakes, crushed

For a bit of colour use chopped pimiento, green or red peppers, if desired. Mix together in big bowl. Pour into greased 9" x 13" pan. Top with dabs of butter and crushed corn flakes. Bake for 2 hours at 200°F.

Mashed Potato Puff

5 lbs.	cooked potatoes, mashed	⅛ tsp.	pepper
		2 tbsp.	butter
6 oz.	cream cheese	1 cup	bread crumbs
1 cup	sour cream	½ cup	butter, melted
1 tsp.	salt		

The day before or a few hours ahead, combine first 6 ingredients and place in 9" x 13" pan. (Refrigerate if not using immediately.) When ready to use, sprinkle bread crumbs over top, then drizzle melted butter over crumbs. Bake in 350°F oven until good and hot. Serve.

Non-Curdling Scalloped Potatoes

2 tbsp.	butter	6 cups	sliced potatoes (not packed)
2 tbsp.	flour		
1½-2 tsp.	salt, or less	1 tbsp.	melted butter
2 cups	milk		

Melt 2 tbsp. of butter in a large saucepan. Stir in flour and salt, then add milk slowly, stirring until sauce thickens. Add potatoes and heat, stirring until sauce boils again. Turn into a greased casserole being sure all potatoes are coated with sauce. Drizzle melted butter over potatoes. Bake, covered, at 350°F for 1 hour or until potatoes are tender. Reduce heat to 325°F and bake for a further 1½ hours.

Note: After the melted butter has been added, the casserole can be refrigerated, covered, until baking time.

Potatoes Romanoff

6	large potatoes	1	bunch green onions, chopped
2-10 oz.	sour cream		
1½ cups	sharp Cheddar cheese, shredded	1½ tsp.	salt
		¼ tsp.	pepper
			paprika

Boil potatoes in jackets until fork tender. Cool. Peel.

Shred potatoes into large bowl. Stir in sour cream, 1 cup shredded cheese, onion, salt, and pepper. Turn into buttered 2-quart casserole.

Top with remaining cheese, sprinkle with paprika. Cover and refrigerate several hours or overnight.

Bake, uncovered, in a 350°F oven about 30 to 40 minutes or until heated through. Makes 8 to 10 servings.

Dill Pickles

fresh cucumbers,		celery
3-4" in length	14 cups	water
fresh dill	¾ cup	vinegar
garlic cloves	½ cup	white sugar
bay leaves	1 cup	pickling salt
carrots		

Wash freshly picked cucumbers in warm water. Fill sink with hot water (water should be hot enough to just hold your hands in.) Place cucumbers in hot water and let them sit until water is lukewarm. Drain.

Place sprig of fresh dill in bottom of each sealer. Pack each sealer with cucumbers. Add 2-3 cloves of garlic, chopped, 1 bay leaf, a carrot and piece of celery to each sealer and top with more dill.

Bring water, vinegar, sugar, and pickling salt to a boil. Cool for 10 minutes then pour over the dills. Steam rubber rings in hot water before putting on sealers, seal tightly. Place sealers in cool place or refrigerator. Let pickles ripen for 10 days before using.

Bread and Butter Pickles

8 qts.	cucumbers, sliced	9 cups	water
2 qts.	onions, sliced	1 cup	salt

Put brine of salt and water over cucumbers and onions and set overnight.

Next day, drain off brine and make syrup.

4½ cups	brown sugar	1 tsp.	celery seed
1½ cups	water	1 tsp.	mustard seed
3½ cups	vinegar	1 tsp.	turmeric

Combine all ingredients. Bring to a boil. Pour over cucumbers and onions and pack in jars. Seal well.

Sauerkraut

| 20 lbs. | cabbage | ½ lb. | pickling salt (⅞ cup) |

Select firm, sound, mature heads of cabbage. Remove outer leaves and wash well. Remove core and slice very finely on cabbage cutter.

Put 5 lbs. (about 7 quarts) shredded cabbage in a crock, add 3½ tbsp. salt, mix well with your hands. Repeat until all cabbage and salt is used. Press down, cover with clean cloth, then with a plate or round wooden board, small enough to fit inside the crock. Weigh down with a clean stone, to keep cabbage covered with brine which forms as the salt draws juice from the cabbage.

Keep in a warm place 75 to 80°F. Inspect each day and, with a spoon, remove the scum that forms. Rinse cloth in clean water and replace. Let stand for 6 or 7 days, until it is sour enough to suit your taste. Put in clean sterilized jars and seal. Put jars in hot water but do not boil, 15 to 20 minutes. Remove jars from the water when they feel quite warm to touch. Store in a cool place.

Sauerkraut

Shred cabbage finely. Pour boiling water over it just to cover. Let stand for 10 minutes.

1 tsp.	pickling salt	2 tsp.	caraway seed
1	bay leaf	½ tsp.	allspice berries
½ tsp.	mustard seed	2 slices	onion

Combine spices, put half of this amount into each jar. Drain cabbage then pack into jars, leave 1½″ of space at the top. Add 1 tsp. vinegar to each jar, then the other half of the spice mixture. Seal tightly and when cool, store in a cold place.

This sauerkraut is ready to eat in 3-4 weeks. Multiply the quantity of spices by the number of jars of sauerkraut you want to make.

Zucchini Pineapple Cocktail

1 gallon	zucchini	48 oz.	can unsweetened
3 tbsp.	pineapple extract		pineapple juice
½ cup	lemon juice		yellow food
3 cups	sugar		coloring

Peel zucchini and cut into squares (large zucchini may be used). Put into large Dutch oven. Add pineapple extract, lemon juice, pineapple juice, sugar, and food coloring. Boil for 10 minutes. Put into hot sterilized jars, seal. Place in hot water bath for 10 minutes.

Makes 5 Quarts.

Saskatoon Berry Jam

6 cups	berries, washed	⅓ cup	lemon juice
1½ cups	water	6 cups	sugar
3 oz.	Certo crystals		

Mash berries slightly, add water, bring to a boil. Add Certo crystals and lemon juice. Stir until mixture comes to a hard boil. Stir in sugar. Bring to a full rolling boil. Boil hard for 1 minute, stirring constantly.

Pour hot mixture into hot sterilized jars and seal immediately.

Freezer Jam

4 cups	raspberries, mashed	4 cups	sugar
3 oz.	pkg. Certo crystals		

Mix raspberries and Certo together and let stand ½ hour, stirring occasionally. Add 4 cups sugar, stir until dissolved. Put into jars. Leave ½" space. Freeze.

Apricot and Pineapple Jam

5 cups	fully ripe apricots	⅓ cup	red marachino or glazed cherries, chopped
14 oz.	can crushed pineapple with juice	3 oz.	box powdered Certo
		6 cups	white sugar

Pit, but don't peel, about 2½ lbs. apricots. Cut into small pieces and grind or chop very fine. Add pineapple and juice. Measure 5 cups combined fruit into saucepan. Add cherries. Measure sugar, set aside. Mix fruit with Certo thoroughly. Place over high heat and stir until mixture comes to a hard boil. Immediately add sugar. Bring to a full rolling boil and boil hard 1 minute, stirring often. Remove from heat. Skim off foam. Stir and cool for 5 minutes. Ladle quickly into glass jars. Cover with melted paraffin wax. Seal.

Baba's Carrot Marmalade

5 cups	carrots, ground	3 cups	sugar
2	oranges	1	small slice fresh ginger root
2	lemons		

Put carrots through meat grinder. Squeeze juice from oranges and lemons, remove inner rind and discard. Grind skins.

Mix all ingredients together including juice. Let stand overnight. Add ginger root to carrot mixture. Simmer on slow burner until carrots are soft and start to stick to bottom of pot. Stir frequently to avoid scorching. Place in jars and seal while hot.

Beet Jelly

3 cups	beet juice	1 pkg.	Kool-Aid
3 oz.	pkg. Certo		(grape is good)
4 cups	sugar		

Cook beet juice, Certo crystals and Kool-Aid for 7 minutes. Add sugar and cook 2 minutes. Put into jars and seal.

Chokecherry Jelly

12 cups	chokecherries	3 oz.	Certo crystals
4 cups	white sugar		

Wash berries. Add enough water to cover berries, and boil until berries are soft. Drain overnight in a jelly bag. Do not squeeze.

To 3 cups chokecherry juice add Certo and sugar. Boil this mixture hard for 1 minute. Pour into hot sterilized jars and seal immediately.

Zucchini Marmalade

6 cups	zucchini, grated	½ cup	lemon juice
4 cups	sugar	14 oz.	crushed pineapple
6 oz.	pkg. peach or apricot Jell-o		

Boil zucchini and sugar for 6 minutes. Add lemon juice and pineapple, boil another 6 minutes. Add Jell-o, stir well. Pour into sterilized jars and seal.

Apple Juice

3 qts.	apples sliced (do not peel or core)	4 tsp.	cream of tartar
		5 qts.	boiling water
		2 cups	sugar

Sprinkle cream of tartar over apples. Pour boiling water over apples. Let set 24 hours.

Strain juice add sugar, taste for sweetness after you add 1½ cups sugar. Put in hot sterilized jars, and seal.

Home-Bottled Rhubarb Juice

3½ qts.	young rhubarb, cut up, clean (about 18 cups)	2 cups	sugar
		½ tsp.	red food colouring
12 cups	hot water		

Into large kettle with cover, measure rhubarb and water, simmer covered for 40 minutes. Strain through fine sieve and measure about 18 cups. Discard purée. Bring juice to a boil and add sugar and food colouring. Bring to a boil again and pour into sterile bottles and seal with screw lids which have been coated on the inside with melted paraffin. This rhubarb does not require dilution with water or ice, but should be served chilled. Makes 4 quarts.

To make a fruit punch using chilled rhubarb juice add an almost equal quantity of chilled canned pineapple juice. Add maraschino cherries and ice cubes to punch bowl when ready to serve.

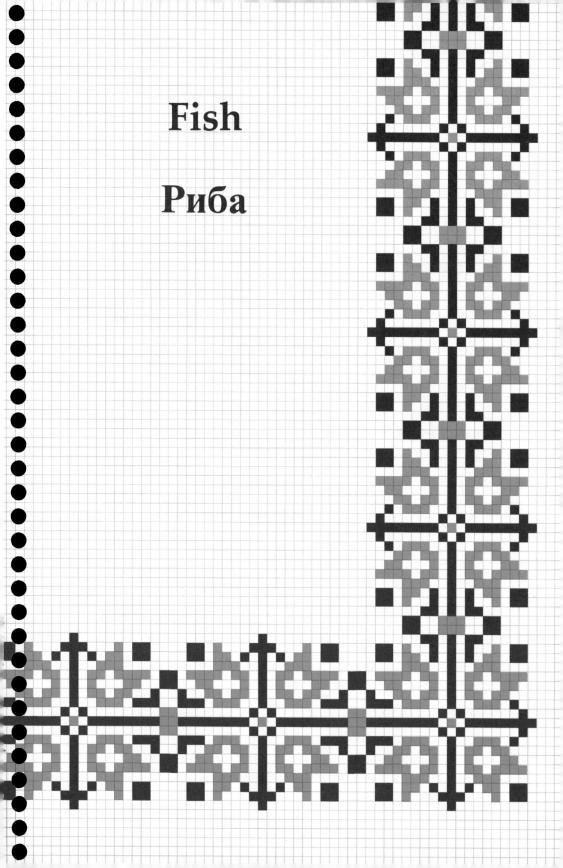

Fish

Риба

Baked Stuffed Salmon

1¾ cups	bread crumbs		⅛ tsp.	pepper
1	small onion, very finely, diced		1 cup	fish stock
1 tbsp.	parsley		1	whole salmon, split down the centre
1 tsp.	sage		6-8	slices bacon
½ tsp.	salt			

Mix first 6 ingredients for stuffing. Stuff the salmon and skewer the fish closed. Lay the stuffed salmon in a buttered baking dish. Pour the stock over the salmon. Place the strips of bacon on top of the salmon.

Bake at 350°F for approximately 15 minutes per pound of salmon.

Serve with hollandaise sauce.

Hollandaise Sauce:

¼ lb.	butter		2 tbsp.	water
2 tbsp.	lemon juice		4	egg yolks

In the top of a double boiler melt the butter, add lemon juice and water. When this is mixed, add the egg yolks (be sure that the top of your boiler does not touch the water underneath). Stir vigorously until thickened. Serve immediately. Do not allow to sit.

If the sauce curdles, remove from heat and add a bit of hot water. Stir vigorously.

Baked Fish Loaf

½ cup	rolled oats	½ tsp.	salt
½ cup	milk	¼ tsp.	pepper
2 tbsp.	mayonnaise	2	eggs, beaten
2 tbsp.	parsley	2 cups	canned salmon,
1	small onion, chopped		drain & save
2 tbsp.	lemon juice		liquid

Combine rolled oats and milk. Add mayonnaise, parsley, onion, lemon juice, salt and pepper. Mix well. Blend in beaten
eggs and fish.

Grease an 8" x 5" loaf pan and press fish mixture into this.
Bake at 375°F for 50-55 minutes.

Unmold on hot platter and pour egg sauce over the top just
before serving.

Egg Sauce:

¼ cup	butter	3	hard-cooked eggs,
¼ cup	flour		finely chopped
1 cup	milk	1 tbsp.	lemon juice
¼ cup	salmon liquid	¼ cup	parsley

Melt butter, stir in flour and cook over low heat until mixture
begins to bubble. Add milk and salmon liquid, stirring constantly until mixture has thickened. Remove from heat, stir in
chopped eggs and lemon juice. Serve over fish loaf.

Garnish with parsley.

Trout Delight

4-10 oz.	trout	¼ cup	margarine
½ cup	flour	1 tbsp.	lemon juice
½ tsp.	salt	12	cooked shrimp, cut
¼ tsp.	pepper		lengthwise
½ cup	peanut oil	1 tsp.	parsley, chopped
2 cups	mushrooms, sliced		

Coat trout with flour, salt and pepper. Sauté in peanut oil until well-browned on both sides. Place on oven-proof platter and heat in 375°F oven for 5 minutes or until done. Sauté mushrooms in same skillet. Stir in margarine, lemon juice and shrimp, heat through. Pour over fish and sprinkle with chopped parsley.

Fisherman's Pie

1 pkg.	haddock fillets, thawed	1½-2 c.	mashed potatoes
1½ cups	milk	2 tbsp.	flour
1	onion, sliced	1 cup	yellow cheese, grated
1	bay leaf	2	eggs, hard-boiled
		2 tbsp.	butter or margarine

Place haddock fillets in shallow pan, cover with milk, onion and add the bay leaf. Cover and bake at 350°F for ½ hour. Strain the milk from the fish and save the liquid. Melt the butter, blend in the flour and add to strained milk. Add grated cheese, cook till thick.

Break up the fish in a pan and pour the cheese sauce over the fish. Slice the boiled eggs and place on the fish in pan. Cover all of this with mashed potatoes. (To the boiled potatoes add 1 raw egg, milk, and margarine. Whip till fluffy.) Bake at 400°F or till golden brown.

Tuna Puff Soufflé

	fine bread crumbs	1	dash cayenne pepper
1/4 cup	margarine	1 1/4 cup	milk
1 cup	mushrooms, thinly sliced	4	egg yolks, well beaten
2	onions, thinly sliced	1 cup	soft bread crumbs
1/3 cup	flour	6 1/2 oz.	can tuna flaked
1/4 tsp.	salt	1 tbsp.	parsley, chopped
1/4 tsp.	dry mustard	4	egg whites

Heat oven to 350°F. Butter a 6-cup souffle dish, sprinkle in some crumbs, shake to coat bottom and sides. Shake out excess.

Melt margarine in medium saucepan over medium heat. Add mushrooms and onions, stir 3 minutes. Sprinkle in next 4 ingredients, stir to blend. Remove from heat, add milk all at once. Return to heat, stir until boiling and thick and smooth.

Gradually stir some of the hot mixture into egg yolk, then stir all back into pan. Remove from heat and mix in bread crumbs, tuna, and parsley. Beat egg whites until stiff but not dry. Fold in tuna mixture and pour into dish. Bake until browned on top and set in middle, about 1 hour. Serves 4-6.

Flaked Fish Ring

2 lbs.	frozen fish fillets, cooked	1 tsp.	salt
2	eggs	1/2 tsp.	pepper
1/2 cup	tomato juice	2 tbsp.	lemon juice
1 1/2 cup	soft bread crumbs	1/4 cup	parsley, minced
		2	celery stalks, chopped

Flake fish. Mix in remaining ingredients. Place mixture in buttered casserole dish and bake in a hot oven, 400°F, for 30 minutes. Serves 6-8.

Cheesy Salmon Supper

15 oz.	canned salmon	¼ cup	carrots, diced
1 tbsp.	lemon juice	½ tsp.	salt
2	eggs, beaten	⅛ tsp.	pepper
1 cup	rolled oats or bread crumbs	½ tsp.	dillweed or parsley flakes
1 cup	Cheddar Cheese, grated	10 oz.	cream of mushroom soup
¼ cup	onion, diced	¾ cup	milk
¼ cup	celery, diced		

Empty salmon with juice into large bowl. Mash and flake well. Sprinkle with lemon juice. Add remaining ingredients, except soup and milk. Blend well.

Spoon into 4½" x 8½" x 3" loaf pan. Bake 30-40 minutes at 350°F until centre is firm. Unmold onto warm platter. Keep hot. Dilute soup with milk, heat and pour over salmon loaf.

Serves 4.

Tuna and Noodles

½ pkg.	Constant noodles, medium	½ tsp.	Worcestershire sauce, (optional)
6½ oz.	canned tuna fish	1 cup	grated cheese
10 oz.	mushroom soup		

Cook noodles for 5 minutes. Mix with other ingredients, except for the grated cheese. Place in greased baking dish. Add grated cheese. Bake in moderate oven for 350°F for 25 minutes.

Shrimp Creole

1	green pepper	½ cup	chicken stock
1	onion, chopped	½ tsp.	salt
1	stalk celery, sliced	¼ tsp.	pepper
4	tomatoes, chopped	2 cups	shrimp, cooked,
4 tbsp.	butter or margarine		peeled
		2-3 cups	rice, boiled

Slice the pepper into strips. Sauté the green pepper, onion, celery and tomatoes in 2 tbsp. butter and cook for 10 minutes. Add stock, salt, and pepper, cook for another 10 minutes. In a smaller pan, sauté the shrimp in 2 tbsp. butter then add to the vegetable mixture. Cook for 2 minutes. Serve on top of boiled rice.

Serves 4.

Shrimp with Chili Sauce

3 tbsp.	oil	1	onion, thinly sliced
½ lb.	shrimp, shelled	¼ tsp.	salt
	and deveined	3 tbsp.	chili sauce

In a wok or fying pan, heat oil to smoking point. Stir-fry shrimp and onions for about 2 minutes. Add salt and chili sauce. Stir everything together and cook 2-3 minutes longer.

Serves 3.

Red Clam Sauce

1	medium-size green pepper, chopped	½ tsp.	oregano
		¼ tsp.	salt
2 oz.	onions, finely, chopped (1 small)	⅛ tsp.	pepper
		8 oz.	canned minced clams, drained
1	clove garlic, minced		
½ cup	clam juice	2 tbsp.	parsley, minced
4	canned medium tomatoes, crushed		

Cook green pepper, onion, and garlic in saucepan over medium-low heat 3 minutes, stirring occasionally. Add clam juice, tomatoes, oregano, salt, and pepper. Bring to boil, then simmer 5 minutes. Add clams and parsley, cook 3 minutes. Serves 4. Wonderful with your favorite pasta.

Tartar Sauce

3 cups	mayonnaise	6 tsp.	chopped onion
12 tbsp.	relish	6 tsp.	chopped parsley
12 tsp.	pimiento	6 tsp.	lemon juice

Combine all ingredients, mix well. May be stored, covered, in refrigerator. Delicious with fish.

Canned Fish

Fill sterilized pint sealers with pieces of raw fish — including bones.

To each sealer add:

½ tsp.	salt	2 tbsp.	oil
2 tbsp.	vinegar	2 tbsp.	ketchup

Process in boiling water for 6 hours.

Meat
and Casseroles

M'ясо

Chicken Kiev

4	medium chicken breasts, split lengthwise and deboned	1 tbsp.	parsley, chopped butter, chilled flour
1 tbsp.	green onions, chopped	2	eggs, beaten
		1 cup	fine bread crumbs

Take deboned and skinned chicken breasts, place between Saran Wrap and pound flat with wooden mallet about ¼" thick. Sprinkle each chicken breast with salt, green onion, and parsley. Place a stick (⅛ of a ¼ lb. stick) of chilled butter on cutlet. Roll the chicken breast up like a jelly roll. Press ends to seal, dust each cutlet with flour, dip into beaten egg, roll in breadcrumbs. Chill for 1 to 2 hours.

Fry in deep, hot fat at 340°F about 5 minutes or until golden brown. Serve with mushroom sauce. This recipe may be made for 2 or 20, adjust quantities accordingly.

Chicken with Wine

1	large chicken (or turkey)	1 pkg.	onion soup mix
		1 pkg.	mushroom soup mix
½ cup	flour	½ cup	sweet wine
½ tsp.	poultry seasoning	1 cup	sour cream
½ tsp.	salt	¼ cup	tomato ketchup
¼ tsp.	pepper		add water if sauce is too thick
1 cup	sliced mushrooms, (optional)		

Cut up chicken or turkey into serving pieces. Dredge in flour, poultry seasoning, salt and pepper combination. Lay in the bottom of a roaster. Top the meat with mushrooms, if desired.

Combine next 6 ingredients. Pour the sauce over the chicken pieces. Bake at 325°F for about 1½ hours. Turn heat off and let stand covered for about 15 minutes. Use sauce for gravy.

*To use with a turkey, this recipe can be doubled. Marvellous for Christmas.

Stir-Fry Chicken with Rice

3	chicken breasts	1	large onion, diced
4 cups	water		(½ cup)
1 tsp.	salt	1	clove garlic, minced
¼ cup	celery leaves,	1 cup	rice, uncooked
	chopped	3 cups	chicken broth
1	bay leaf	½ tsp.	salt
1	small onion	¼ tsp.	pepper
1-2 tbsp.	soy sauce	½ cup	peas, frozen or
10 oz.	can mushrooms,		fresh
	sliced		

Debone chicken breasts. Cook bones in salted water with celery leaves, bay leaf and small onion for about 45 minutes. Strain, reserving broth. Cut chicken in ½" strips. Pour soy sauce over and marinate for about 1 hour.

In electric frypan, or stainless steel pan with lid, stir-fry chicken in 1 tbsp. of oil on high heat. Add drained mushrooms, diced onions, garlic and fry for a few minutes longer. Add the uncooked rice, chicken broth, salt and pepper to taste. A little more soy sauce may be added, if desired. Turn down heat. Cook about 15-20 minutes with lid on. Stir several times. Add peas and cook another 8-10 minutes.

Chicken and Rice Casserole

1 cup	uncooked long-	10 oz.	can mushroom soup
	grained rice	10 oz.	water
1	chicken, cut up	1	pouch (38 g) Lipton
½ tsp.	salt		Onion Soup mix
¼ tsp.	pepper		

Put the rice in the bottom of a casserole. Lay the chicken pieces on top of the rice. Sprinkle with salt and pepper. Combine the soups and water. Pour this soup mixture over the chicken. Make sure that the water gets down to the rice. Cover and cook at 325°F for about 2 hours. Uncover for the last ½ hour to brown the top, if desired.

Orange-Glazed, Rice-Stuffed Cornish Game Hens

6 oz.	Uncle Ben's Long-grain and Wild Rice	2	Cornish Game hens, thawed
1	bay leaf	½ cup	orange juice
10 oz.	mushroom stems and pieces	4	sticks celery, cut in 1" chunks
1	small onion, chopped	½ lb.	carrots, cut in 1" chunks
2 tbsp.	butter or margarine or oil	1 tbsp.	butter or margarine, melted
½ tsp.	salt	2 tbsp.	flour, blended with ¼ cup water
¼ tsp.	pepper		

Cook rice per package directions, add bay leaf to water. In skillet sauté mushrooms and onions in butter until lightly browned. Stir in cooked rice, salt, and pepper to taste. Discard bay leaf. Sprinkle body cavities of hens with salt and pepper. Spoon rice mixture lightly into cavities; skewer with toothpicks; tie legs. Place orange juice, celery, and carrots in roaster; top with hens, cover and bake in 375°F oven for 1½ hours, until fork-tender. Remove cover, brush with melted butter, bake 10 minutes or until browned. If desired, pour pan juices into small saucepan. Stir flour mixture into pan juices, cook and stir over medium heat until thickened. Split hens lengthwise and serve with stuffing and vegetables. Makes 4 servings.

Country Captain

½ cup	flour	1-2	cloves garlic,
1 tsp.	salt		finely chopped
¼ tsp.	pepper	28 oz.	can tomatoes
2½-3	chicken cut into	1 tsp.	salt
lbs.	serving pieces	1 tsp.	curry powder
½ cup	butter or margarine	1 tsp.	thyme
½ cup	oil	1 tsp.	chopped parsley
1	medium onion,	½ tsp.	white pepper
	thinly sliced		
1	green pepper,		
	thinly sliced		

Combine flour, salt, and pepper and dust chicken pieces in this mixture. Sauté chicken in the butter and oil until golden brown. Place chicken in casserole.

Melt 1 tbsp. butter in saucepan and sauté the onion, green pepper, and garlic for 10 minutes. Add the tomatoes and remaining ingredients and cook another 10 minutes. Pour over chicken in casserole. Cover tightly and cook in 350°F oven for 45 minutes or until chicken is tender.

Sweet and Sour Chicken

1	frying chicken

Cut chicken into serving pieces, place in a small roaster.

Sauce:

1½ cups	brown sugar	1	beef cube (Oxo)
½ cup	vinegar	3 tbsp.	corn starch
1 cup	water		

Combine all ingredients in a saucepan. Bring to a boil, then pour over the chicken. Bake at 350°F for 1½ hours or until meat is done.

Serve with rice.

Chicken in Sour Cream

7-11	chicken breasts, halved	20 oz.	can cream of mushroom soup
1 tbsp.	butter	1½ oz.	pkg. dry onion soup mix
1 tsp.	salt		
1 tsp.	pepper	2 cups	dairy sour cream
1 tsp.	paprika	1 tbsp.	lemon juice
		1 tsp.	dillseed

Place chicken in buttered baking dish. Dot each piece with butter, sprinkle with salt, pepper and paprika. Combine remaining ingredients and pour over chicken.

Bake in 350°F oven for 1¼ to 1½ hours or till chicken is tender and sauce is brown.

Serve with rice and vegetable salad.

Other chicken pieces could be used.

Sour Cream Chicken Casserole

4 oz.	corned beef	8	slices bacon
8	half chicken breasts skinned and deboned	2 cups	sour cream
		10 oz.	can cream of mushroom soup

Grease casserole. Place 2 pieces corned beef on each chicken breast, roll up, wrap with bacon. Pin with a toothpick. Combine sour cream and soup, pour over breasts. Bake at 300°F for 3 hours.

Paupiettes (Rolled Round Steak)

1-2 lbs.	¼" thick round steak		dill pickles
	prepared mustard	½ tsp.	salt
	precooked bacon	¼ tsp.	garlic salt
	strips	¼ tsp.	pepper

Cut steak into 3 — 4" squares. Spread mustard on each slice of meat. Place bacon on steak slice. Wrap steak around dill pickles that have been sliced into quarter sections. Fasten rolls with toothpicks. Season rolls with salt, pepper, and garlic salt. Brown rolls in a skillet and arrange in a casserole. Make gravy with the meat stock from browning rolls.

Gravy:

2 tbsp.	flour	1 cup	liquid, (water
½ tsp.	salt		or beef broth)
2 tbsp.	drippings		

Add flour and salt to pan drippings. Cook for a few seconds. Slowly add liquid, simmer until thickened.

Sauce:

½ cup	onion, diced	1 tsp.	parsley flakes
2	cloves garlic, finely	1 oz.	dry red wine
	chopped		

Combine all ingredients with gravy. Pour over paupiettes in casserole. Bake at 350°F for ½ hour.

Mustard Sauce

| 2 tbsp. | dry mustard | ⅓ cup | vinegar |
| ½ cup | white sugar | 1 | egg, well-beaten |

Combine dry mustard and sugar. Add vinegar slowly, mixing in. Add egg. Cook slowly over low heat or in double boiler till it thickens. Delicious with ham, pork, sausages, etc.

Beef Stroganoff

½	medium onion, chopped	1 tsp.	Worcestershire sauce
1 tbsp.	butter	½ tsp.	salt
2½ lbs.	sirloin steak		Noodles
1 cup	mushrooms, quartered	3 tbsp.	flour
		1 cup	water
10 oz.	can consommé	¾ cup	sour cream

Prepare steak by cutting into strips 3″ x 1″ x ¼″, trimming away all fat, gristle, and bone. In frying pan sauté onion in butter until translucent. Add meat and sear, turning constantly, 4-5 minutes. Remove from heat. Add mushrooms, consommé, Worcestershire sauce, and salt. Meanwhile, cook noodles. 5-6 minutes before serving time, heat contents of pan to boiling. Make a smooth paste of flour and water and stir until thickened. Add sour cream and heat mixture thoroughly. Drain noodles and serve stroganoff over them.

Katherine's Meat Roll

	milk	8 oz.	lean veal, ground
2	slices dry white bread	4	egg yolks
		½ tsp.	pepper
4 oz.	butter, melted	1 tsp.	salt
8 oz.	ham, finely chopped or ground		

Soak the bread in milk and squeeze out well. Mix all ingredients, including egg yolks, into 1 mass. Shape into an oblong form and wrap in a well-buttered cloth. Tie ends with string. Place in oblong container filled with hot water and boil slowly for 1 hour.

Cool and remove the cloth. When cold, slice and place on platter lined with lettuce. Garnish with sliced tomatoes and mayonnaise to serve.

Marinade for Corned Beef

For 1-4 lbs. of beef brisket:

8 tsp.	pickling salt	4		cloves garlic
4 tbsp.	mixed whole pickling spice	½ cup		brown sugar
		1 cup		cold water
3 tsp.	saltpeter			

Mix above ingredients together. Marinate corned beef in refrigerator for 7 days. Turn meat over daily. After 7 days, wash meat off and cook according to your favorite recipe.

Pork Sausage

10 lbs.	fresh ground pork	2 tsp.	sage
3 tbsp.	salt	4 cups	cold water
1 tsp.	cayenne pepper	2 cups	flour
½ tsp.	saltpeter		pork casings
1½ tsp.	black pepper		

Combine all ingredients, mix thoroughly. Stuff casings, then twist sausage length to form individual sausages. Fry in a greased pan, turning to brown on all sides. Serve at once. These are also great on the barbecue. (Pork sausages freeze well.)

Pork Sausage Stuffing

1 lb.	pork sausage meat	4 cups	bread crumbs
1-1½ c.	water	1 tsp.	salt
¼ cup	butter	¼ tsp.	pepper
½ cup	celery, finely cut	1½ tsp.	sage
1	medium onion, finely chopped		

Boil sausage meat with water to cover until it looses its colour. Save the water. Combine butter, celery, onion, fry until soft. Combine all ingredients, mix well. Use as stuffing for chicken or turkey. Will stuff a 6-8 lb. bird.

Sweet and Sour Spareribs

2 lbs.	spareribs	1-2	Spanish onions, sliced

Roast spareribs with Spanish onions for approximately 1 hour at 350°F. Drain off fat.

Sauce:

2 tbsp.	flour	1 cup	water
1 cup	brown sugar	2 tbsp.	soya sauce
¾ cup	vinegar		(or more, if desired)

When mixing sauce, mix flour with brown sugar first, then stir in the vinegar, and other ingredients. Cook sauce until thickened and pour over the ribs. Return to oven for 15 minutes at 350°F.

Barbecued Spareribs

3½-4 lb.	spareribs cut into 1 rib pieces	3 tbsp.	sugar
¾ cup	ketchup	3 tbsp.	vinegar
2 tbsp.	Worcestershire sauce	⅓ cup	water
		¾ tsp.	salt
		⅛ tsp.	garlic salt

Prepare the sauce first by mixing all ingredients, except for ribs, in a bowl and letting them stand.

1½ hours before mealtime, put cut up ribs on a rack in a large shallow pan and roast at 350°F for 1 hour. Then drain off all fat. Remove rack. Give sauce a good stir and spoon over ribs. Return to oven and bake at 350°F for ½ hour longer, turning ribs once.

Desserts
and Pastries

Десерт,
Солодощі

Jean's Poppy Seed Cake

1 cup	buttermilk	1 tsp.	vanilla
¼ cup	poppy seeds	2½ cups	flour
½ cup	margarine	2 tsp.	baking powder
½ cup	shortening	1 tsp.	baking soda
1½ cups	white sugar	4	egg whites, stiffly
4	egg yolks		beaten

Soak poppy seeds in buttermilk for 1 hour. Cream together margarine, shortening, sugar, egg yolks, and vanilla. Combine dry ingredients, blend into creamed mixture alternately with milk. Gently fold egg whites into batter.

Filling:

⅓ cup	granulated sugar	2 tsp.	cocoa
1 tsp.	cinnamon		

Spoon about ⅓ of batter into a greased bundt pan. Sprinkle over ½ of the sugar-cocoa mixture. Spoon in another ⅓ of the batter, top with remaining sugar-cocoa mixture, then add remaining batter. Cut through with a knife to marble layers. Bake at 350°F for 1 hour, until wooden pick inserted in centre comes out clean.

Bundt Poppy Seed Cake

½ lb.	poppy seeds	¾ tsp.	soda
7	eggs, separated	½ tsp.	salt
1½ cups	sugar	1½ cups	bread crumbs, finely
1 cup	oil		crushed
2 tsp.	baking powder	½ cup	walnuts, chopped

Cover the poppy seeds with water and cook for ½ an hour. Grind by putting through a blender. Beat the egg yolks adding the sugar gradually while beating. Then add the oil, baking powder, soda, salt, bread crumbs and poppy seed, beating after each addition. Beat egg whites till stiff and then fold in. Gently stir in the walnuts. Bake in a large bundt pan at 350°F for 60 minutes.

See photograph page 130.

Sylvia's Poppy Seed Cake

1 cup	dry poppy seed	2 cups	flour
6	eggs	2 tsp.	baking powder
2 cups	sugar	1/8 tsp.	salt
1¼ cups	corn oil	1 cup	walnuts
½ cup	milk	½ cup	cherries

Pour boiling water over poppy seed. Drain and dry on towels. Beat eggs with sugar. Add oil and beat. Add poppy seed, milk, flour, baking powder, salt and walnuts. Mix well. Pour into greased and floured 9" x 13" pan or 2, 9" round pans. Top with cherries. Bake for 1 hour at 325°F.

See photograph page 130.

Poppy Seed Walnut Torte

1¼ cups	poppy seed	1 cup	granulated sugar
1 cup	walnuts	1 tsp.	vanilla
10	eggs, separated		

Grind poppy seed and walnuts. Beat egg yolks until creamy, gradually add sugar and beat until thick.

Mix in ground poppy seeds and walnuts, add vanilla, fold in stiffly beaten egg whites. Pour into round 9" cake pans, greased and floured.

Bake at 350°F for 30 minutes. Leave cakes in pans and cover with cloths for 1 day.

Filling:

5 tbsp.	milk	⅜ lb.	butter
1 cup	sugar	1 cup	whipping cream, whipped
½ lb.	ground walnuts		

Heat milk and sugar over low heat until sugar is dissolved. Remove from heat, add walnuts. Cool, add butter. Whip until light and fluffy. Spread filling between torte layers. Top with whipped cream.

Torte

6	eggs, separated	½ tsp.	allspice
1 cup	sugar	½ tsp.	cloves
1 cup	almonds, ground	1 tsp.	cinnamon
1 cup	fine bread crumbs	1 tsp.	baking powder
1	orange, juice and grated rind		

Beat egg yolks until light. Add sugar and beat 5 minutes. Add almonds and mix. Combine bread crumbs with orange juice and grated rind. Add spices and baking powder. Beat egg whites until stiff and fold into the above mixture.

Grease 2, 10″ springform pans with lard, coat with bread crumbs. Spoon the batter into the prepared pans. Bake at 350°F for 30 minutes, or until done. Allow the cake to stand in pans for 5 minutes and then remove to a cake rack, until completely cool (like angel food cake). Spread any favorite filling between the layers and over the sides.

Soft Honey Cake

½ tsp.	salt	6	eggs, separated
1 tsp.	baking powder	½ cup	granulated sugar
1 tsp.	baking soda	½ cup	Mazola oil
1 cup	flour (can be a 50/50 mixture of regular flour and cake flour	½ cup	honey, liquified
		¼ tsp.	cream of tartar
		1 tsp.	vanilla

Combine first 4 ingredients and sift 3 times to ensure a good mixture. Beat egg yolks with wooden spoon to a light colour. Add sugar gradually while beating the egg yolks. Mix oil with liquified honey then mix with sugar mixture stirring in 1 direction.

Separately add cream of tartar to egg whites and beat to a stiff foam. Add vanilla to egg yolks. Add dry ingredients gradually and mix well. Finally add egg whites and fold in thoroughly. Bake at 300°F in a greased 9″ x 13″ pan for 1 hour.

Orange-Honey Cake

½ cup	butter, unsalted	1 tsp.	baking powder
1 cup	brown sugar, firmly packed	1 tsp.	baking soda
		½ tsp.	salt
4	eggs, separated	1 tsp.	cinnamon
1 cup	buckwheat honey	¼ tsp.	ground cloves
1 tsp.	vanilla	¼ tsp.	nutmeg
2 tbsp.	orange rind, grated	1 cup	walnuts, chopped
		1 cup	strong cold coffee
3 cups	all-purpose flour	½ cup	orange juice

Cream together butter and brown sugar, beat in egg yolks, 1 at a time, and continue beating until batter is light. Stir in honey, vanilla, and orange rind.

Sift together flour, baking powder, soda, salt, and spices. Remove 2 tbsp. of sifted mixture and toss with walnuts, set aside. Beat dry ingredients into creamed mixture in 3 parts, alternating first with coffee and then with orange juice. Stir nuts into batter just until evenly distributed.

Beat egg whites until stiff, fold into batter. Transfer to greased and floured 10" tube or bundt pan, bake in 300°F oven for 1½ hours, until deep amber and firm to touch. Cool in pan on rack, ideally, let mature for 2 days before slicing. Dust with icing sugar if desired, serve on a doily-lined cake plate or stand. Makes about 16 servings.

Chocolate Chip Date Cake

1½ cups	boiling water	1½ cups	flour plus 2 tbsp.
1 cup	dates, finely chopped	½ tsp.	salt
1 tsp.	soda	2 tsp.	baking powder
½ cup	margarine	½ cup	brown sugar
1 cup	sugar	½ cup	chocolate chips
2	eggs	½ cup	walnuts, chopped

Pour water over dates add soda and cool. Beat together margarine, sugar, and eggs. Combine dry ingredients, mix into sugar mixture. Add date mixture. Pour batter into greased pan 9" x 12". Sprinkle with brown sugar, chocolate chips and walnuts. Bake at 350°F for 35-40 minutes.

Never-Fail Chiffon Cake

7	egg whites	¾ cup	water
½ tsp.	cream of tartar	3 tsp.	baking powder
1½ cups	sugar	2 cups	flour
½ cup	oil		rind of 1 lemon,
7	egg yolks		grated
1 tsp.	lemon juice		

Beat egg whites and cream of tartar together until stiff. Cream sugar and eggs, until light and fluffy. Add egg yolks one at a time beating well after each addition. Add water, lemon juice, rind and oil, beat well after each addition. Combine flour and baking powder. Fold egg yolk mixture into flour mixture. Fold in stiffly-beaten egg whites. Pour into greased angel food pan. Bake at 325°F for 55 minutes, until cake springs back when touched. Cool in pan.

Variations:

Nut Cake: Add ½ cup finely chopped nuts.
Spice Cake: Add 1 tbsp. cinnamon, ½ tsp. each, nutmeg, cloves, and allspice.
Poppy Seed Cake: Add 2 tbsp. poppy seed.

Raspberry Honey Cake

¾ cup	honey	2 cups	flour
½ cup	brown sugar	½ tsp.	salt
½ cup	margarine	1 tsp.	baking soda
2	eggs	1 cup	buttermilk
1 tsp.	vanilla	1½-2 c.	raspberries

Combine honey, brown sugar, margarine, eggs, and vanilla. Beat well. Sift flour with baking soda and salt. Add alternately with buttermilk, mix until well blended. Fold in raspberries. Pour into a greased and floured 9" x 13" pan. Bake at 350°F for 35 minutes. Frost with butter icing page 131. For a pink color add raspberry juice.

See photograph page 130.

Pear Nut Torte

1	egg	¼ tsp.	salt
¾ cup	sugar	2	large ripe pears
2 tbsp.	flour	½ cup	chopped nuts
1 tsp.	baking powder	1 tsp.	vanilla

Beat egg and sugar together until very light. Mix flour, baking powder, and salt. Stir into the egg mixture. Peel pears and dice into large pieces. Combine with the batter. Add nuts and vanilla. Bake in a buttered 8″ square pan at 350°F for 35 minutes. Serve with cream, whipped cream, or ice cream.

You may substitute apples for the pears. Add a little cinnamon and omit the nuts.

Cherry Cake

6 oz.	red maraschino cherries	1 cup	brown sugar
		⅔ cup	milk
6 oz.	green maraschino cherries	2	eggs
		⅓ cup	butter, melted
2½ cup	all-purpose flour, sifted	½ cup	chopped walnuts
		1 tbsp.	orange rind
4 tsp.	baking powder	½ cup	icing sugar
½ tsp.	salt	2 tbsp.	milk

Drain cherries, reserving red syrup. Cut cherries in half. Sift dry ingredients together. Combine red cherry syrup, milk, eggs, butter. Stir into flour mixture until mixed but still lumpy. Fold in cherries, nuts, and rind until well-blended.

Turn into greased 9″ x 5″ loaf pan. Bake at 350°F 60-70 minutes or until done. Remove from oven.

Combine icing sugar, and milk. Pour over hot loaf, cool. If storing do not glaze.

Sandra's Orange Cheesecake

Crumb Crust:

2½ cups	fine graham wafer crumbs	½ cup	plus 1 tbsp. butter, melted
		⅓ cup	white sugar

Mix graham wafer crumbs, butter, and sugar together. Press into a buttered springform pan and bake 5 minutes at 350°F, cool.

Filling:

2 tbsp.	plain gelatine	3	eggs, separated
¼ cup	lemon juice	1 tsp.	orange rind, grated
¼ cup	cold water	8 oz.	cream cheese, room temperature
⅔ cup	sugar		
⅛ tsp.	salt	1 cup	whipping cream
½ cup	fresh orange juice		

Soak the gelatine in lemon juice and water for 5 minutes. Stir together in top of double boiler with sugar, salt, and orange juice. Heat, stirring, over boiling water until gelatine and sugar dissolve. Beat egg yolks and stir some of the mixture into them. Return all to double boiler and cook, stirring, until mixture thickens slightly. Remove from heat. Add orange rind and cool. Beat in cream cheese, adding small lumps of it at a time until all is incorporated and mixture is smooth. Beat egg whites until stiff and fold into the mixture. Whip cream till stiff then fold into the mixture to make a smooth blend. Pour into crumb crust. Chill overnight.

Orange Glaze:

10 oz.	can mandarin oranges	2 tbsp.	cornstarch or arrowroot flour
¼ cup	sugar	½ cup	fresh orange juice
¼ tsp.	salt	½ tsp.	yellow food coloring

Drain and dry mandarin oranges, saving juice. Arrange in attractive circles around the edge and at center of chilled cheesecake, combine dry, ingredients in saucepan. Stir in fresh orange juice. Measure the juice from the canned mandarin oranges. Make it up to ⅔ cup by adding boiling water to the canned juice. Stir into the orange juice mixture and cook, stirring until thick. Reduce heat and cook 2-3 minutes longer. Remove from heat, add food coloring. Spoon over the top of the cake and orange sections, then drizzle small amounts down the sides of the cake.

Quick No-Bake Cheesecake

3 oz.	pkg. lemon Jell-o	½ pt	whipping cream
1 cup	boiling water	1 tsp.	vanilla
1-2 tbsp.	sugar	9	graham wafers
8 oz.	Philadelphia cream cheese	¼ cup	graham crumbs

Beat first 4 ingredients together until smooth. Whip cream until stiff, add vanilla. Pour lemon mixture into whipped cream and beat together. Pour into 8" x 8" pan lined with graham wafers. Sprinkle crushed wafer crumbs on top. Chill overnight in refrigerator.

Dream Cake

½ cup	butter	½ tsp.	salt
1 cup	flour	1 tsp.	sugar

Cut butter into dry ingredients until fine like crumbs. Spread into 8" x 8" greased pan and bake 15 minutes at 350°F.

2	eggs	1 tsp.	vanilla
1 cup	brown sugar	1 tsp.	baking powder
1 cup	chopped nuts	2 tbsp.	flour
½ cup	fine coconut	10-12	maraschino cherries

Cream eggs and sugar, stir in nuts, coconut, and vanilla. Combine baking powder and flour. Add to batter. Stir in cherries. Spread this on crust and bake 15 to 20 minutes at 350°F. Remove from oven, cool in pan.

Cheesecake Dessert

Crust:

2 cups	graham wafer crumbs	6½ tbsp.	brown sugar
		6½ tbsp.	butter

Combine all ingredients. Line bottom of 8″ x 8″ pyrex cake pan with ¾ of crumb mixture. Save ¼ of the crumbs for top of the dessert. Bake in 350°F oven for 10 minutes. Do not overbake. Cool.

Instead of baking the crust may be chilled in the refrigerator while preparing filling.

Filling:

3 oz.	pkg. Dream Whip, whipped	1 cup	icing sugar
8 oz.	pkg. Philadelphia cream cheese	19 oz.	can cherry pie filling

Whip the Dream Whip, let stand in refrigerator for 10 minutes. Whip cream cheese and icing sugar and fold in the whipped Dream Whip. Spread over cooled crust and let stand in refrigerator for 15-20 minutes.

Spread cherry pie filling over cheese mixture and sprinkle remaining crumbs on top. Blueberry pie filling may be used if desired.

Whipped Shortbread

½ cup	cornstarch	½ lb.	butter
3 cups	flour	½ lb.	margarine
1½ cups	icing sugar		

Sift cornstarch, flour, icing sugar. Blend butter and margarine with dry ingredients. Beat well. Drop batter from teaspoon on ungreased cookie sheet. Decorate as desired. Bake at 350°F for 15 to 20 minutes.

See photograph page 130.

Pineapple Cheesecake

2½ cups	graham wafer crumbs	1 tsp.	vanilla
½ cup	butter, or a little more, melted	19 oz.	can crushed pineapple
1 lb.	cream cheese	2 cups	sour cream
1 cup	sugar	½ tsp.	vanilla
3	eggs		

Mix crumbs with butter. Spread in bottom of a 12½″ x 8½″ pyrex pan, leaving a little to sprinkle on top. Cream cheese and sugar well, add eggs, 1 at a time, and vanilla. Beat until smooth. Pour over crumbs. Bake in 325°F oven for ½ hour.

Drain pineapple well — add sour cream and vanilla and mix. Place pineapple mixture carefully over baked cheese layer. Sprinkle remaining crumbs over cake and put back into oven for about 5 minutes.

See photograph page 130.

Pineapple Slice

2½ cups	vanilla wafers, finely rolled	½ cup	melted butter

Combine wafers and butter. Mix well. Reserve ½ cup crumbs. Press into a greased 9 x 13″ pan, bake for 15 minutes at 325°F. Cool.

½ cup	butter	1½ cups	icing sugar, sifted
2	eggs		

Cream butter and sugar, add eggs, beat lightly with egg beater. Pour evenly over vanilla wafer mixture.

19 oz.	can crushed pineapple, well-drained	1 cup	heavy whipped cream

Fold pineapple into whipped cream. Spread over egg mixture. Top with the remaining wafer crumbs. Chill for several hours.

125

Lemon Loaf

½ cup	butter		rind of 1 lemon,
1 cup	sugar		finely grated
2	eggs, beaten	½ cup	walnuts, chopped
½ cup	milk		(optional)
1½ cups	flour		juice of 1 lemon
1 tsp.	baking powder	¼ cup	sugar
1 tsp.	salt		

Cream butter and sugar. Add beaten eggs and milk. Add dry ingredients, no sifting required, lemon rind, and walnuts. Mix well, bake in 9" x 5" greased loaf pan for 1 hour at 350°F. Remove from oven, cool for 5 minutes. Combine lemon juice and sugar. Pierce the cake with a fork, pour juice over loaf. Allow to stand at least 1 hour before removing from pan.

Pumpkin Loaf

¾ cup	cooking oil	1 tsp.	baking powder
1 cup	sugar	1 tsp.	baking soda
2	eggs	1 tsp.	cinnamon
1 cup	pumpkin, mashed	½ cup	raisins
	or canned	¼ cup	walnuts, chopped
1½ cups	flour, sifted		(optional)
½ tsp.	salt		

Combine oil with sugar, then beat in eggs and pumpkin. Sift dry ingredients, add raisins and nuts and stir into pumpkin mixture. Turn into a greased loaf pan and bake 1½ hours at 350°F. If desired, drizzle with thin frosting made of icing sugar mixed with milk or cream. Makes 1 loaf, about 9" x 5" x 3".

Chocolate Zucchini Loaf

3	eggs	3 cups	all-purpose flour
2 cups	granulated sugar	1 tsp.	salt
1 cup	salad oil	1 tsp.	cinnamon
2 oz.	unsweetened	1½ tsp.	baking powder
	chocolate, melted	1 tsp.	baking soda
1 tsp.	vanilla	1 cup	almonds, sliced
2 cups	zucchini, grated, unpared		

In mixer bowl beat eggs until lemon coloured. Beat in sugar and oil. Stir in melted chocolate. Add vanilla and grated zucchini. Sift together flour, salt, cinnamon, baking powder, and soda. Add to the first mixture. Fold in nuts.

Pour into 2, 9" x 5" x 3" greased loaf pans. Bake at 350°F for 60 minutes. Cool in pans for 15 minutes. Turn out onto rack to cool.

Date Loaf

1 tsp.	baking soda	½ cup	nuts, chopped
1 cup	dates	1½ cups	flour
1 cup	boiling water	2 tbsp.	butter
1 cup	white sugar	½ tsp.	salt
1	egg	1 tsp.	vanilla

Sprinkle soda over dates and pour boiling water over them. Let cool and add remaining ingredients. Mix well, bake in 9" x 5" loaf pan at 350°F oven about 40 minutes. Slice and serve buttered.

Fruit Cake

1 cup	fresh unsalted butter	6	eggs
1 cup	sugar	⅔ cup	seedless white raisins
2 cups	flour	⅓ cup	mixed fruit
3 tsp.	baking powder		rind of 1 lemon, grated
1 tsp.	salt	½ cup	rum

Cream softened butter with sugar till smooth. Slowly add flour, baking powder, salt, and 1 egg at a time, stirring in one direction till all dry ingredients and eggs are used up. Add and stir in raisins, dry fruit, rind, and finally, rum.

Divide batter into 2 narrow well-greased pans lined with wax paper, fill each pan just over the halfway mark. Bake at 350°F for 1 hour. To preserve, store in refrigerator without removing the wax paper.

Light Fruit Cake

2⅔ cups	flour	1½ cups	white raisins
1 tsp.	salt	1½ cups	slivered, blanched almonds
1 tsp.	baking powder		
3 cups	shredded coconut	2 cups	sugar
1½ cups	candied cherries, cut in halves	1 cup	butter
		4	eggs
1½ cups	candied pineapple, diced	1 tsp.	almond extract
		1 cup	pineapple juice

Line 9" x 10" tube pan with 2 thicknesses of buttered brown paper.

Measure flour into large bowl. Add salt and baking powder, stir well to blend. Add coconut, fruits, and nuts. Mix until fruit is separated and coated with flour. Cream sugar, butter, eggs, and almond extract thoroughly. Stir in fruit-flour mixture alternately with pineapple juice, starting and ending with fruit-flour mixture.

Spread batter evenly in prepared pan. Bake at 275°F for 3 to 3½ hours. Keep a pan of hot water in oven while baking. Leave in pan to cool. Remove paper liner and wrap in foil. Store in refrigerator or cool place.

Christmas Cake

4½-5 c.	flour	1 cup	sugar
2 tsp.	baking powder	7	eggs
1 tsp.	salt	½ cup	corn syrup
1 tsp.	nutmeg	19 oz.	can drained,
1 lb.	glazed cherries, cut		crushed pineapple
	in halves	¼ lb.	candied pineapple,
2 cups	citron peel		chopped
1½ lb.	sultana raisins	½ cup	brandy
½ lb.	bleached sultana	1 tsp.	vanilla
	raisins	1 tsp.	almond extract
6 oz.	blanched and		
	shredded almonds		
1½ cups	butter		

The amount of flour required will depend on the softness of batter due to the amount of liquid in the pineapple. Use smaller amount of flour, adding the extra half cup only if batter seems to be rather thin. Prepare bread pans by lining them with brown paper and grease well.

Measure flour, baking powder, salt, and nutmeg, set aside. Combine fruit, dust with flour, mixture, minus 1 cup.

Beat butter until creamy and light, add sugar gradually, beating between additions. Then add eggs, one at a time, unbeaten; beating each one in thoroughly before adding next. If mixture curdles, add a little flour mixture, then continue to add the eggs. Add pineapple, syrup, brandy and flavouring. Add flour and fruit mixture. Fill prepared pans ¾ full.

Bake in 275°F to 300°F oven for 3 to 3½ hours. Place pan of water in oven. When cake cools it may seem crisp. Before storing, rub about ½ cup brandy over cakes. Wrap in wax paper and cheesecloth. Store in cool place. Let ripen about 6 weeks, then try. If you feel it's ready, it can now be frozen to keep.

Yields: about 4 loaves. About 10 lbs.

See photograph page 130.

Plum Coffee Cake

¾ cup	sugar	6-8	fresh Italian
½ cup	butter		plums, pitted
1	egg		and sliced
1 tsp.	vanilla	½ cup	brown sugar
1¼ cup	flour		firmly packed
2 tsp.	baking powder	3 tbsp.	flour
½ tsp.	salt	½ tsp.	cinnamon
½ cup	milk	3 tbsp.	melted butter
		¼ cup	chopped nuts

Cream together sugar, butter, egg, and vanilla. Sift together flour, baking powder, and salt. Alternately add milk and dry ingredients to butter mixture. Spread dough in a greased 9″ square pan. Top with rows of plum slices, skin side down. Combine remaining ingredients until crumbly, not smooth, and sprinkle over plums.

Bake in a preheated 375°F oven for 35 minutes or until done. Cut into squares.

Rhubarb Cake

1½ cups	brown sugar	1 tsp.	vanilla
½ cup	margarine	1½ cups	rhubarb, diced
1	egg	½ cup	white sugar
1 cup	sour cream	1 tsp.	cinnamon
1 tsp.	soda	1 tsp.	flour
2 cups	flour		

Cream together sugar, margarine, beat in egg. Add sour cream. Combine dry ingredients, mix in. Add vanilla then rhubarb. Mix well and put in greased 9″ x 12″ pan. Combine white sugar, cinnamon, and flour. Sprinkle topping over batter.

Bake at 350°F for 30 minutes.

Desserts

1. Ukrainian Torte (p. 56)
2. Syrnyk Cheesecake (p. 34)
3. Christmas Cake (p. 129)
4. Kalyna (Cranberry) Pyrizhky (p. 58)
5. Bublyky (Cream Puffs) (p. 135)
6. Pineapple Cheesecake (p. 125)
7. Coconut Dainties (p. 146)
8. Yeast-Raised Rohalyky (Crescents) (p. 57)
9. Rosalyn's Poppy Seed Slice (p. 142)
10. Raspberry Honey Cake (p. 120)
11. Chocolate Chip Slice (p. 145)
12. Scuffles (p. 153)
13. Whipped Shortbread (p. 124)
14. Bundt Poppy Seed Cake (p. 116)
15. Apple Pie Slice (p. 146)
16. Mary's Good Slice (p. 148)
17. Graham Wafer Cake (p. 145)
18. Sylvia's Poppy Seed Cake (p. 117)
19. Cherry Square (p. 147)

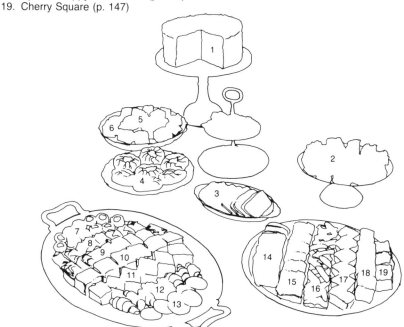

Chocolate Torte Filling

2 sqs.	unsweetened chocolate	1 cup	icing sugar
		2	egg yolks
½ cup	salt-free butter	1 cup	walnuts, ground

Melt chocolate and cool. Beat butter with electric mixer. Add sugar and egg yolks, beat. Add chocolate and beat again, add walnuts. A nice torte filling.

Chocolate Glaze

2 tbsp.	butter	1¼ cups	icing sugar
2 sqs.	unsweetened chocolate	1	egg
		1 tsp.	vanilla

Melt butter and chocolate. Whisk in remaining ingredients until smooth. Spread over cake.

Vanilla Butter Icing

4 tbsp.	butter	½ tsp.	vanilla
2 cups	icing sugar, sifted	3 tbsp.	milk or cream

Cream butter until very soft. Add sugar gradually, blending thoroughly. Add vanilla. Add milk or cream, a little at a time, until you have the right consistency.

Mocha Whipped Cream

1½ cups	whipping cream	1 tbsp.	instant coffee
3 tbsp.	icing sugar	2 tsp.	unsweetened cocoa

Whip cream until soft peaks form. Gradually beat in sugar, coffee, and cocoa. Beat until stiff.

White Whipped Frosting

1 cup	cold milk	1 cup	white sugar
2 tbsp.	corn starch	1 tsp.	vanilla
½ lb.	soft margarine (1 cup)		

Cook milk and cornstarch until thick, stirring constantly. Chill in refrigerator for ½ hour.

In big beater bowl combine margarine, sugar, and vanilla. Beat until snowy white. Add the sauce from the refrigerator. Beat for 15 minutes until sugar granules disappear.

This is not sweet and makes a large recipe.

Forever Icing

4	egg whites	1 cup	shortening
4 cups	icing sugar	1 tsp.	vanilla

Beat egg whites until peaks hold, beat in icing sugar gradually, then beat in shortening and vanilla until fluffy, about 15 minutes. Store up to 6 months in freezer. Cakes iced with this frosting may be frozen.

Freezer Icing

5 tbsp.	flour	1 cup	shortening
1 cup	milk	1 tsp.	vanilla
1 cup	white sugar		

Cook flour and milk until thick, stirring constantly, cool. Cream sugar and shortening. Add vanilla. Beat until fluffy and add to cool flour mixture. Beat until it looks like whipped cream. Spread on cake. This frosts 2 large cakes. Freezes very well.

Pumpkin Roll

¾ cup	flour	3	eggs
1 tsp.	baking powder	1 cup	sugar
2 tsp.	cinnamon	⅔ cup	pumpkin
1 tsp.	ginger	1 tsp.	lemon juice
¼ tsp.	nutmeg	¾ cup	walnuts, finely
¼ tsp.	salt		chopped

Sift together first 6 ingredients. Beat eggs for 5 minutes until thick. Gradually beat in 1 cup sugar. Stir in pumpkin and lemon juice. Fold dry ingredients into pumpkin mixture. Spread in well-greased 10″ x 15″ cookie sheet. Sprinkle top with nuts. Bake at 325°F for about 20 minutes. Take out of oven. Loosen edges. Turn out immediately onto a towel which has been sprinkled with icing sugar. Roll towel and cake together. Let cool for 1 hour. Unroll and spread with filling.

Filling:

1 cup	sugar	4 tbsp.	butter
6 oz.	cream cheese	½ tsp.	vanilla

Beat all ingredients together spread over jelly roll and roll up again.

Peach Pudding

3-4	medium peaches,	½ cup	milk
	sliced	1 cup	flour
¾ cup	sugar	⅛ tsp.	salt
1	egg	1 tsp.	baking powder
2 tbsp.	shortening	1 tsp.	vanilla

Butter a 9″ glass pie plate. Fill with sliced peaches. Combine remaining ingredients and pour over peaches. Bake at 350°F for 30 minutes or until cake tester inserted in center comes out clean.

Strawberry Trifle

6 oz.	pkg. strawberry jelly powder		14 oz.	angel cake
2 cups	boiling water		1 cup	whipping cream
1 cup	strawberry syrup, from frozen berries		2 tbsp.	sugar
2-15 oz.	pkgs. frozen strawberries, thawed and drained		1 tsp.	plain gelatin
			1 tbsp.	water

Custard Topping:

6 tbsp.	all-purpose flour	or use Birds Custard
¾ cup	granulated sugar	to replace this
⅜ tsp.	salt	custard topping
2½ cup	warm milk	
3	egg yolks, lightly beaten	
1½ tsp.	vanilla	

Dissolve jelly powder in boiling water. Stir in 1 cup of strawberry syrup reserved from strawberries. Let jelly cool slightly.

Cut cake into 1¼" squares. Place ⅓ of the cake pieces in a very large bowl. Pour ⅓ of the liquid jelly over the cake. Cover with ½ the strawberries. Repeat with another ⅓ of the cake pieces, ⅓ liquid jelly and last ½ of the fruit. Cover with remaining cake and pour remaining jelly over this. Press down lightly to let cake absorb more of the liquid. Let set in refrigerator.

To make Custard Topping: Combine flour, sugar, and salt in top of double boiler. Warm milk in small saucepan and stir into dry ingredients mixing thoroughly so there are no lumps. Add a little of this mixture to the beaten egg yolks, mixing well. Return to hot mixture in double boiler. Cook slowly, stirring constantly until thickened. Remove from heat and stir in vanilla. Cover and allow to cool. When cooled, spoon over top of the jellied fruit and cake mixture, then refrigerate.

Close to serving time, prepare whipped cream: In a cup, combine the water and plain gelatin and let soak a few minutes. Stand cup in boiling water and stir to dissolve. Remove from heat and cool slightly but not too much or it will gel. Pour whipping cream and sugar into a bowl and beat at high speed. When cream has just begun to thicken, pour in gelatin liquid, slowly, while beaters are still on. Beat until stiff. Top custard with whipped cream. Decorate top of whipped cream, if desired, with slivered almonds, whole or sliced strawberries, cake sprinkles, etc.

Serves 10 generously.

Bublyky (Cream Puffs)

½ cup	butter	1 cup	flour
⅛ tsp.	salt	4	eggs
1 cup	water		

Add butter and salt to water, bring to the boiling point. Add flour, cook mixture until it leaves the side of the pan, cool. When nearly cold, add unbeaten eggs, 1 at a time.

Drop mixture by the spoonful on a buttered cookie sheet, leaving space for rising.

Bake in moderate oven, 350°F for 40 minutes.

When cold, split, fill with whipped cream, top with chocolate syrup.

See photograph page 130.

Raisin Dumpling Pudding

Sauce:

½ cup	brown sugar	4 cups	boiling water, or
1 tbsp.	butter		3 cups boiling
1 tsp.	vanilla		water and 1 cup
			cold coffee

Mix sauce ingredients and boil for 15 minutes.

Batter:

1 tbsp.	butter	½ cup	sweet milk
½ cup	white sugar	1 cup	flour
2 tsp.	baking powder	½ cup	raisins

Cream butter and sugar add remaining ingredients. Mix well. Pour into hot syrup. Bake at 350°F, until batter has risen and is baked golden brown, about 30 minutes.

Raspberry Dessert

20	graham wafers, rolled fine	15 oz.	pkg. frozen raspberries
¼ cup	brown sugar	20 lg.	marshmallows (white)
¼ cup	butter		
3 oz.	pkg. raspberry Jell-o	½ cup	hot milk
1 cup	boiling water	1½ cups	whipped cream

To graham wafer crumbs add brown sugar and butter. Mix well. Line 9" x 13" pan, saving 1 cup of mixture for topping.

Dissolve the raspberry Jell-o in 1 cup boiling water. Add the frozen raspberries and mix well. Melt the marshmallows in the hot milk until all are dissolved. Cool. Add the whipped cream.

Put raspberry Jell-o mixture on crumbs and then spread marshmallow and cream mixture over them. Sprinkle the cup of crumbs on top. Refrigerate overnight.

Tart Pastry

2 cups	flour	1 cup	shortening
3 tsp.	baking powder	½ cup	milk
2 tbsp.	sugar	1 tsp.	vanilla
¼ tsp.	salt		

Cut shortening into the first 4 ingredients until crumbs are formed. Add milk and vanilla, mix well; roll out dough on lightly floured surface to ⅛" thickness, cut into 5" circles. Press circle into 3½" tart shells. Bake in 425°F oven 12 minutes or until golden brown. Cool, fill as desired or omit baking, fill and then bake according to your filling recipe.

Pie Crust

5 cups	flour	1 lb.	lard
2 tbsp.	sugar	1	egg
1 tsp.	baking powder	⅔ cup	water, ice cold
½ tsp.	salt	1 tbsp.	vinegar

Mix flour, sugar, baking powder, salt and cut in lard. Beat egg and mix with water and vinegar. Then add flour mixture. Chill. May be frozen for future use.

Pie Crust

4½ cups	flour	1 cup	hot water
4 tsp.	baking powder	1	egg
2 tsp.	salt	4 tsp.	lemon juice
2 cups	shortening		

Dissolve ⅔ cup shortening in hot water. Cut 1⅓ cups shortening into flour until crumbs are formed. Add the egg and lemon juice, then add hot water mixture to the crumb mixture. Mix well. Place in refrigerator to cool.

Coconut Tarts

2	eggs, beaten	1 cup	unsweetened fine
1 cup	sugar		coconut
1 tbsp.	butter, melted	¼ cup	jam, flavor
1 tsp.	coconut or		of your choice
	vanilla flavoring		

Blend together the first five ingredients. Line small tart pans with unbaked tart crust. Put ½ teaspoon of jam in the centre of shell. Put 1 teaspoon coconut filling on top of jam. Bake at 375°F for 20 minutes.

Yields 24.

Honey Tarts

2	eggs	¼ tsp.	salt
½ cup	honey	1 tsp.	vanilla
¼ cup	sugar	⅔ cup	pecans

Beat eggs, add honey, sugar, salt, vanilla, and pecans. Pour into unbaked shells, bake in 400°F oven for 15 to 18 minutes.

Pecan Pie

¼ cup	butter or margarine	3	eggs
½ cup	sugar	1 cup	pecan halves
1 cup	dark corn syrup	1	9″ unbaked
¼ tsp.	salt		pastry shell

Cream butter and sugar until light and fluffy. Add syrup and salt and beat well. Add eggs, one at a time, beating after each. Stir in pecans. Pour into pastry shell. Bake at 350°F for 50 minutes. Pie is done when knife inserted in centre comes out dry.

Cool before serving with ice cream.

Rum Pie

Shell:

1 tbsp.	shortening	6 oz.	semisweet chocolate chips

Line a glass pie plate with foil, smoothing the foil wrap so there are no creases. Add shortening and chocolate chips, melt in a 325°F oven for 10 minutes. With a spatula, smear melted chocolate and shortening over the bottom and sides of the foil, until it forms a pie shell. If the chocolate is too runny, let it cool slightly. Chill the chocolate shell in the refrigerator. When firmly chilled, carefully peel away foil and rest chocolate shell back in the pie plate or on a serving platter.

Filling:

6 egg	yolks	⅓ cup	dark rum
¾ cup	white sugar	2 tbsp.	chopped pistachio nuts or shaved chocolate
1 tbsp.	powdered gelatin		
½ cup	cold water		
2 cups	whipping cream, whipped		

Beat egg yolks until light. Add sugar and mix. Soften gelatin in cold water, dissolve over low heat in double boiler. Bring just to a boil, add the egg yolks, stir briskly. Let cool, then fold in whipped cream, then rum. Pour into chocolate shell and sprinkle with pistachio nuts or shaved chocolate. Chill. Serves 6-8.

Butter Tart Filling

½ cup	brown sugar	1	egg, beaten
¼ cup	corn syrup	3 tbsp.	butter
½ cup	raisins	1 tsp.	vinegar
1 tsp.	vanilla or rum		salt

Combine all ingredients in heavy saucepan, mix well and bring to a boil. Boil until thick and pour into baked tart shells.

Rhubarb Custard Pie

1 cup	sugar	3 cups	rhubarb
2 tbsp.	minute tapioca	1	9" unbaked
2	egg yolks		pastry shell
1 cup	creamilk or		
	condensed milk		

Blend sugar, tapioca, egg yolks, and cream. Chop rhubarb finely and put into unbaked pie shell. Pour custard mixture over rhubarb. Bake at 400°F for 15 minutes. Reduce heat to 325°F until custard sets, about 45 minutes.

Meringue:

2	egg whites	½ tsp.	lemon extract
1 tbsp.	sugar		

Beat egg whites until stiff, add sugar, lemon extract and spoon over baked pie, sealing meringue to crust. Return to 325°F oven and bake until meringue is golden, about 10-15 minutes.

Sour Cream Raisin Pie

1	egg, beaten		pinch of salt
1 cup	sugar	½ tsp.	vanilla
1 cup	sour cream	1	9" unbaked
1 cup	raisins		pastry shell

Beat the egg, add the sugar and beat until the sugar is partially dissolved, add cream, raisins, salt, and vanilla. Blend and pour into unbaked pie shell. Bake at 400°F for 10 minutes, then 350°F till done, about 40 minutes. Pie is done when knife inserted in centre comes out dry.

Mincemeat

1½ lbs.	raisins		1 tsp.	cinnamon
1 lb.	apples, peeled, cored		½ tsp.	allspice
			⅛ tsp.	salt
1 lb.	currants		¼ lb.	mixed peel
¾ lb.	sultanas		½ cup	rum, more or less to your taste
1 lb.	chopped suet			
1 lb.	sugar			

Put raisins and apples through a food chopper, add other ingredients, mix well, put in jars and seal, or put in containers and freeze.

Marshmallow Squares

½ cup	butter		2 tbsp.	cocoa
1 cup	sugar		½ cup	walnuts, coarsely chopped
2	eggs, beaten			
¾ cup	flour			

Cream butter and sugar. Add beaten eggs. Add flour sifted with cocoa. Stir in walnuts. Spread in jelly roll pan. Bake at 350°F for 15 minutes.

2 tbsp.	plain gelatine		¾ cup	boiling water
½ cup	cold water		½ tsp.	salt
2 cups	white sugar		1 tsp.	vanilla

Soften gelatine in cold water. Boil sugar and boiling water together until a thread forms when dropped from edge of spoon. Remove from heat. Add gelatine to hot syrup and stir well to mix. Add salt and vanilla. Beat with electric mixer until mixture becomes thick, cold, and fluffy. Pour onto cake base, let set until firm. Ice with chocolate glaze, page 131.

Rosalyn's Poppy Seed Slice

1 tsp.	yeast	¼ tsp.	salt
1 tsp.	sugar	4 tbsp.	sugar
½ cup	warm milk	½ lb.	or 1 cup shortening
3 cups	flour	2	egg yolks, beaten
1 tsp.	baking soda		

Dissolve yeast and sugar in milk, about 10 minutes. Sift dry ingredients together, cut in shortening. Rub together as you would for pastry. Make a well in the mixture, add yeast mixture and egg yolks. Mix until all ingredients are blended and you then have a soft dough. Divide the dough into 3 equal portions. Cover and set aside.

Poppy Seed Filling:

2 cups	poppy seed	3 tbsp.	flour, to make a
1½ cups	sugar		soft paste
1 cup	hot water	1 tsp.	vanilla extract

Grind poppy seeds, add remaining ingredients. Blend all the ingredients together and set aside while you prepare the dough for the baking sheet.

Roll out 1 layer of dough (large enough to fit a cookie sheet — approximate size 16″ x 11″). Then spread ½ of the poppy seed mixture on this first layer of dough. Roll out the second portion of dough. Place on top of poppy seed filling. Then cover the second layer of dough with the balance of the poppy seed mixture. Roll out the third portion of dough and place on the poppy seed mixture.

Place in a warm area, cover and let rise for 1 hour.

Bake in a 325°F oven for 45 minutes. Remove from oven and let cool. Then frost with the following butter icing.

Butter Icing:

1 cup	icing sugar		cream
1½ tbsp.	soft butter	1	square semisweet
⅛ tsp.	salt		chocolate

Blend sugar, butter, salt, adding enough cream to make a soft texture. Spread on cooled slice. Melt 1 square of semisweet chocolate. Drizzle the chocolate lengthwise making parallel lines about 1″ apart. Then pull a fork, lightly, across the chocolate the opposite way, if desired.

Cut the slice in finger-length pieces, approximately ¾″ x 2″.

See photograph page 130.

Lemon Squares

½ cup	butter	4 oz.	lemon pie filling
2 tbsp.	icing sugar	½ tsp.	baking powder
1 cup	flour	1 cup	chopped dates
2	eggs, well-beaten	1½ cup	coconut
½ cup	sugar		

Mix first 3 ingredients together. Mix well, spread in 8″ x 8″ pan and bake 15 to 20 minutes at 350°F. Mix remaining ingredients together. Spread over crust. Bake at 350°F about 25 minutes until lightly browned.

Spanish Peanut Slice

1 cup	margarine	12 oz.	butterscotch chips
¾ cup	brown sugar	2 tbsp.	oil
1½ cups	flour	1 tbsp.	water
¾ cup	syrup	2 cups	Spanish peanuts

Mix margarine, sugar, and flour thoroughly, then press into a 9″ x 12″ pan. Bake at 375°F for 10 minutes.

Combine syrup, chips, oil and water in a heavy saucepan and melt over low heat. Stir until dissolved and creamy. Take off heat. Add Spanish peanuts. Pour over the crust mixture. Put in refrigerator.

Carob Brownies (Low Sugar)

½ cup	butter or margarine, softened	⅓ cup	whole wheat pastry flour
⅓ cup	brown sugar	2 tsp.	baking powder
½ tbsp.	vanilla	6 tbsp.	carob powder
2	eggs, lightly beaten	1 cup	chopped walnuts or pecans
4 tbsp.	water		
⅛ tsp.	salt (optional)		

Cream together butter or margarine and sugar, in a medium-sized mixing bowl. Mix in vanilla, eggs, and water. Sift together salt, flour, and baking powder, and stir slowly into butter-sugar mixture. Stir in carob powder and the nuts (save a few nuts to decorate top of cake), mixing well. Grease and flour an 8″ x 8″ cake pan and fill evenly with batter. Place whole nuts on top if desired. Bake brownies in preheated 350°F oven for 25 minutes.

Makes 16.

Brownies

1½ cups	flour	1 cup	oil
1 tsp.	salt	4	eggs
2 cups	sugar	¼ cup	cold water
½ cup	cocoa	½ cup	walnuts, chopped
2 tsp.	vanilla		

Put all ingredients in a large bowl in order given. Beat at low speed, scraping down sides of bowl, until smooth. DON'T BEAT TOO LONG. Grease a 13″ x 9″ x 2″ pan and pour batter into it. Push the batter into the corners and smooth the top. Bake at 350°F for 30 minutes — no longer. If glass pan is used, bake at 325°F for 30 minutes. When cool, ice with chocolate frosting, sprinkle with chopped walnuts.

Chocolate Chip Slice

1 cup	chopped dates	½ tsp.	salt
1 tsp.	baking soda	1 tsp.	vanilla
1 cup	boiling water	1½ cups	flour
½ cup	butter	2 tbsp.	cocoa
½ cup	Mazola Oil	⅔ cup	chocolate chips
1 cup	white sugar	½ cup	walnuts, chopped
2	eggs, beaten		

Combine dates, soda, and boiling water, cool. Cream together butter, oil, and sugar. Add eggs, salt and vanilla.

Sift together flour and cocoa. Add the flour mixture alternately with the date mixture to the creamed mixture. Pour into 9″ x 13″ greased pan. Sprinkle with chocolate chips and chopped walnuts. Bake at 375°F for about 45 minutes or until toothpick comes clean.

See photograph page 130.

Graham Wafer Cake

⅓ cup	butter		pinch of salt
1 cup	sugar	1 tsp.	baking powder
2	eggs, well-beaten	1½ cups	coconut
30	graham wafers, crumbed	1 cup	milk
		½ tsp.	vanilla

Cream butter and sugar, add eggs. Mix graham wafer crumbs, salt, baking powder, and coconut. Add alternately with milk and vanilla to creamed mixture. Spread in 9″ x 13″ pan. Bake in 350°F oven for 30 minutes.

Icing:

1 cup	brown sugar		thicken with icing
½ cup	plus 2 tsp. butter		sugar
		½ tsp.	almond flavouring (optional)

Beat together icing ingredients, spread over cooled cake.

Apple Pie Slice

2½ cups	flour	1 cup	cornflakes, crushed
1 cup	Tenderflake lard	6-8	apples, peeled,
1	egg yolk in cup,		sliced
	add cold milk	1	egg white
	until ⅔ full	½ cup	icing sugar
1 cup	sugar	2 tbsp.	water
1 tsp.	cinnamon		

Cut lard into flour. Mix in egg and milk mixture. Mix as for pie crust. Dough will be soft. Place in refrigerator for 30 minutes before rolling.

Divide dough in half. Roll ½ in rectangular shape to fit 15" x 10" cookie sheet and roll into pan.

Sprinkle crushed cornflakes over dough. Place apples on top of dough. Combine sugar and cinnamon and sprinkle on apples. Roll out second ½ of dough, place over apples. Beat egg white till stiff. Brush on top. Prick dough with a fork as for a pie. Bake for 30-40 minutes at 350°F, until golden.

While still warm, mix icing sugar with water and drizzle over top. Cool. Cut into squares. Freezes well.

See photograph page 130.

Coconut Dainties

8 oz.	cream cheese	1 cup	fine shredded coconut
	softened	1 cup	flaked coconut
4 cups	icing sugar	12 oz.	package mints

Beat cheese and icing sugar well. Add coconut. Shape into small balls in the palm of your hands. Place on waxed paper and make a dent in center with a coloured mint. Keep in refrigerator till cold. These freeze well. Makes 100 dainties.

See photograph page 130.

Cherry Square

1 cup	soft margarine or butter	2 cups	flour, not sifted
1 cup	granulated white sugar	1 cup	walnuts, chopped
1 tsp.	vanilla	19 oz.	can pie filling (cherry, peach blueberry, or raspberry).
2	eggs		

Mix margarine or butter with sugar. Beat in vanilla and eggs. Add flour and nuts. Stir or beat just to mix.

You will need a 13″ x 9″ pan. If glass, grease it, if not, don't. Spread ¾ of the batter evenly in pan. Now spread pie filling over the batter. Drop remaining batter at random by teaspoonful over filling. This should cover ¾ of the surface. Bake at 325°F for 45 minutes.

Note: Leftovers can be stored in refrigerator. Do not cover when storing. If covered when stored, the filling may soak the base.

See photograph page 130.

Chocolate Refreshers

1¼ cups	sifted flour	½ cup	butter
¾ tsp.	baking soda	1 cup	chocolate chips
½ tsp.	salt	2	eggs
1¼ cups	dates, cut up	½ cup	orange juice
¾ cup	brown sugar, firmly packed	½ cup	milk
½ cup	water	1 cup	walnuts, chopped

Sift flour with soda and salt. Combine dates, brown sugar, water, and butter in large sauce pan. Cook over low heat, stirring constantly until dates soften. Remove from heat. Stir in chocolate chips. Beat in eggs. Add dry ingredients alternately with orange juice and milk. Blend thoroughly after each addition. Stir in walnuts. Bake in well-greased jelly roll pan at 350°F for 25 minutes. Cool. Ice with butter icing, page 131.

Prune Platsok

6 tbsp.	butter	2½ cups	flour
4	egg yolks (use whites for meringue	3 tsp.	baking powder
½ cup	sugar	½ cup	sweet cream

Cream together butter, egg yolks, and sugar. Add flour, baking powder and cream. Mix ingredients together and press into greased and floured 10″ x 12 ″ pan.

1½ lbs.	prunes	1 tsp.	cinnamon
½ cup	sugar	1 tsp.	lemon juice

Cook prunes. Drain and remove pits. Add sugar, cinnamon to taste and lemon juice. Mix well. Spread prune mixture on dough. Cover with the egg white topping.

Egg White Topping

4	egg whites	3 tbsp.	sugar
1 tbsp.	water	½ tsp.	baking powder
3 tbsp.	cornstarch	1 tsp.	vanilla

Beat egg whites until stiff. Beat in remaining ingredients. Spread meringue on top of prune mixture. Bake in 325°-350°F oven for 40 to 50 minutes.

Mary's Good Slice

2 cups	flour	½ cup	sugar
½ tsp.	baking powder	1	egg
½ tsp.	baking soda	½ cup	sour cream
⅛ tsp.	salt	19 oz.	can pie filling
½ cup	margarine		

Mix flour, baking powder, baking soda and salt together. Cut in margarine. Add remaining ingredients, except for pie filling, as for pie crust. Press ¾ of dough into 9″ x 12″ pan. Spread pie filling over base.

Roll out remaining dough, cut into strips for lattice topping and apply strips to form a diamond pattern. (for a glaze, brush top with a slightly beaten egg). Bake at 350°F for 25-30 minutes.

See photograph page 130.

Peanut Honey Oat Cookies

½ cup	margarine	1 cup	flour
½ cup	peanut butter	1½ tsp.	baking powder
⅓ cup	brown sugar	½ tsp.	salt
¼ cup	honey, liquid	½ cup	rolled oats
1	egg	½ cup	chopped peanuts
1 tsp.	vanilla		(optional)

Cream margarine, peanut butter, brown sugar, and honey. Add egg and vanilla. Beat well. Sift together flour, baking powder and salt. Add to creamed mixture, mixing well. Stir in rolled oats and peanuts.

Drop from a teaspoon onto a greased and floured cookie sheet. Bake at 375°F for about 10 minutes. Yields 4 to 5 dozen.

Crackle-Top Peanut Butter Cookies

¾ cup	margarine	1 tsp.	vanilla
¾ cup	sugar	1¾ cups	all-purpose flour
¾ cup	brown sugar, packed	½ tsp.	baking soda
1	egg	½ tsp.	salt
¾ cup	peanut butter,	½ cup	granulated sugar
	smooth or	1 tbsp.	vanilla sugar
	crunchy		

Cream margarine and sugars. Beat in egg, peanut butter, and vanilla. Add flour sifted with baking soda and salt. Mix well. Chill 20-30 minutes. Form into round balls, roll in sugar and vanilla sugar mixture and place on ungreased pan. Do not flatten. Bake at 375°F for 10-12 minutes. Makes 5 dozen.

Mushroom Cookies

4	eggs	¾ cup	oil (Crisco or
1 tbsp.	sugar		Mazola)
¼ tsp.	salt	1 cup	all-purpose flour

Beat eggs well with the sugar. Add salt and oil and beat again until bubbles show. Add the sifted flour and beat well until light and bubbly.

Use a muffin tray with small round-shaped cups, curled bottoms. Place ½ tsp. of oil into each cup. Using a teaspoon drop 1 tsp. of batter into each muffin cup.

Bake at 375°F for 28-30 minutes. Test with finger, dough will not yield to light pressure.

During baking, the batter puffs up the sides of the tin, leaving the centre empty, resembling a "mushroom".

When cool, they may be filled with whipped cream if desired. Top with cherry (optional). May also be filled with cooked apricot filling.

Brown Sugar Drop Cookies

1⅔ cups	all-purpose flour	1½ cups	brown sugar,
1 tsp.	baking powder		lightly packed
1 tsp.	baking soda	2	eggs
¼ tsp.	salt	1 tsp.	vanilla
¾ cup	margarine		nuts or candied
			cherries

Sift together first 4 ingredients. Cream margarine, sugar, add eggs, and vanilla blend well. Add flour mixture, blend well. Drop by teaspoon, well apart, on a greased and floured cookie sheet. Top each with nut or cherry. Bake in 325°F oven 10-12 minutes. Let stand 1 minute, cool on wire racks. Makes 3½ dozen.

Butterscotch Oatmeal Cookies

½ cup	brown sugar, packed	1 tsp.	salt
½ cup	granulated sugar	½ tsp.	baking powder
½ cup	butter or margarine	½ tsp.	baking soda
1	egg	1 cup	quick-cooking
1 tbsp.	milk		rolled oats
1 tsp.	vanilla	1 cup	butterscotch-
1 cup	all-purpose flour		flavoured chips

Cream sugars, and butter together until light and fluffy. Add egg, milk, vanilla. Sift together flour, salt, baking powder and baking soda. Add flour mixture, blend well. When smooth, add rolled oats and butterscotch chips. Drop 2″ apart on well-greased cookie sheet and bake at 350°F until light brown. Makes 3 dozen cookies.

Crescent Cookies

½ cup	butter	1¾ cups	pre-sifted flour
½ cup	shortening	¾ cup	finely chopped nuts
½ cup	icing sugar	¾ cup	semisweet chocolate
1 tsp.	vanilla		bits

Preheat oven to 375°F. Cream butter, shortening, and sugar with vanilla until light and fluffy. Blend in flour gradually. Add nuts and mix well.

Pinch off small balls of dough. Roll into finger lengths and shape into crescents.

Bake on lightly-greased cookie sheets in 375°F oven for 15 minutes or until lightly browned. Cool. Melt chocolate and dip ends of each crescent in the chocolate. Place on rack to set chocolate. Makes 3½ dozen approximately.

Gingersnaps

2 cups	flour	¾ cup	butter or margarine
¼ tsp.	salt	1 cup	sugar
2 tsp.	baking soda	1	egg
1 tsp.	cinnamon	¼ cup	molasses
1 tsp.	ground cloves	½ cup	sugar
1 tsp.	ground ginger	1 tbsp.	vanilla sugar

Sift flour, salt, baking soda, and spices together. Cream butter and sugar. Add egg and molasses then dry ingredients. Mix well. Form into small balls, roll in ½ cup white sugar mixed with vanilla sugar. Place on greased cookie sheets. Bake at 350°F for 10-12 minutes.

Honey Cookies

2 cups	honey	2 tbsp.	lemon juice
4 tsp.	baking soda	1 cup	milk
2 cups	sugar (1 white,	½ tsp.	salt
	1 brown)	1 tbsp.	dry yeast dissolved
4	egg yolks		in ¼ cup warm
½ lb.	butter, softened		milk
		8 cups	flour

Heat honey, add soda, let cool. Mix egg yolks and sugar together. Beat in butter, lemon juice, milk, salt, and dissolved yeast. Add flour, mix well. Put in refrigerator overnight, well-covered. Roll out to about ½'' thickness, cut with cookie cutters. Bake till brown in 350°F oven, about 15 minutes.

Raisin Drop Cookies

2 cups	raisins, boiled in ½ cup water until tender, cooled	2	eggs
		2 cups	flour
		1 tsp.	baking powder
1 cup	brown sugar	1 tsp.	baking soda
1 cup	lard or half margarine or butter, melted	1 tsp.	cinnamon
		½ tsp.	cloves
		½ tsp.	allspice

Cream sugar with lard, beat in eggs. Combine remaining ingredients, stir into egg mixture. Add raisins and mix well. Roll dough into small balls. Put on greased cookie sheets. Press with fork and bake at 350°F till nicely browned, about 12-15 minutes.

Scuffles

2 tbsp.	yeast	½ cup	warm water
2 tsp.	sugar		

Dissolve yeast and sugar in water, about 10 minutes.

2 cups	butter or margarine	1 cup	milk
6 cups	flour	4	eggs, beaten
⅓ cup	white sugar	2 cups	sugar
½ tsp.	salt	4 tbsp.	cinnamon

Cut butter into flour, sugar and salt. Add yeast. Stir in milk and eggs. Mix and chill in refrigerator overnight.

Mix sugar with cinnamon. Roll out dough into circles, about 9" in diameter and about ¼" thick. Sprinkle sugar mixture on both sides of dough. Cut in wedges as you would a pie and roll up from the wide end to the narrow end. Place on greased cookie sheets. Bake for 15 minutes at 350°F.

Makes about 15 dozen, depending on size made.

See photograph page 130.

Jam Buns

¾ cup	butter		2 tbsp.	sugar
2 cups	flour		4 tsp.	baking powder
¼ tsp.	salt		½ cup	milk
1	egg			jam

Cut butter into flour and salt. Cream egg and sugar together. Add baking powder to flour. Stir flour mixture into egg mixture, alternately with milk. Mix like pie crust. Roll out and cut into squares. Put tsp. of jam in centre and pinch corners together. Bake in muffin tins in 350°F oven for 25 minutes or until lightly brown.

Elephant Ears

8 egg	yolks		1 tbsp.	any liqueur or
4	whole eggs			dark rum
1 tsp.	salt		⅛ tsp.	baking powder
2 tsp.	vanilla		4-5 cups	flour (enough to
1 tbsp.	sugar			make stiff dough)

Combine first 6 ingredients, mix well. Add baking powder to flour, mix into egg mixture.

Cover, let stand for ½ hour, roll out dough on floured surface. Cut long strips of dough, about 1" wide, then cut the strips on a bias about 2" long, in triangular shapes. Make a slit in the middle and twist the pointed end through. Fry in hot oil, drain on paper towels. Do not freeze, they keep well in a dry place. When serving, sprinkle with icing sugar.

Metric Aid For The Kitchen

To remember metric measures:

mL (millilitre) is used for measuring liquid or dry ingredients in most recipes
cm (centimetre) is used for measuring cookie sheets and thickness of meat
L (litre) is used for volume such as soup pots and casseroles
kg (kilogram) is a unit of mass — not weight — used for shopping for large and/or heavy items
C (degree Celsius) is the metric measure for temperature
g (gram) is a unit of mass used in shopping for light or small items.

Metric quantities:

100 g	is a little less than ¼ lb.
250 g	is a little more than ½ lb.
500 g	is a little more than 1 lb.
1 kg	is a little more than 2 lb.
2 kg	is a little more than 4 lb.
3 kg	is a little more than 6 lb.
	1000 g = 1 kg

Temperature replacement chart:

150°C	=	300°F
160°C	=	325°F
180°C	=	350°F
190°C	=	375°F
200°C	=	400°F
220°C	=	425°F
230°C	=	450°F
260°C	=	500°F

Metric Conversion Table

Volume Measure

		exact	rounded
1 tsp.	=	(5 mL)	5 mL
3 tsp.	= 1 tbsp. =	(14.2 mL)	15 mL
4 tbsp.	= ¼ cup =	(56.8 mL)	50-60 mL
5⅓ tbsp.	= ⅓ cup =	(75.6 mL)	75 mL
8 tbsp.	= ½ cup =	(118.25 mL)	125 mL
16 tbsp.	= 1 cup =	(236 mL)	250 mL
1 fl. oz.	= 2 tbsp. =	(29.56 mL)	30 mL
4 fl. oz.	= ½ cup (1 gill) =	(118.25 mL)	125 mL
8 fl. oz.	= 1 cup =	(236 mL)	250 mL
16 fl. oz.	= 2 cups (1 pint) =	(473 mL)	500 mL
32 fl. oz.	= 4 cups (1 quart) =	(946 mL)	1000 mL (1 L)

Weight Measure

		exact	rounded
1 oz.	= ¹⁄₁₆ lb. =	(28.3 g)	30 g
4 oz.	= ¼ lb. =	(113.4 g)	125 g
8 oz.	= ½ lb. =	(226.8 g)	250 g
16 oz.	= 1 lb. =	(453 g)	500 g
32 oz.	= 2 lbs. =	(917.2 g)	1000 g (1 kg)

Members and Recipe Contributors

ANAKA, Mrs. Helen
ANTHONY, Mrs. Verna
ARYCHUK, Mrs. Eftima
BABCHUK, Mrs. Nettie
BATRYN, Mrs. Mary
BEAHUN, Mrs. Pearl
BOBOWSKY, Mrs. Sylvia
BOJUK, Mrs. Lena
BOYCHUK, Mrs. Elizabeth
BREMNER, Mrs. Sonia
CHELAK, Mrs. Paraska
CHEREPUSCHAK, Mrs. Lesia
CVASNETA, Mrs. Martha
CZEMERES, Mrs. Katie
DUMANSKI, Mrs. Marge
DUSYK, Mrs. Mary
FEKULA, Mrs. Elsie
GREGORY, Mrs. Dora
HARRAS, Mrs. Sharon
HLECK, Miss Mary Ann
HLECK, Mrs. Mary Lou
HLUCHANIUK, Mrs. Iris
HLYNSKI, Mrs. Stella
HNEDA, Mrs. Anne
HNEDA, Mrs. Helen
HOLOWACH, Mrs. Vi
HRYCAY, Mrs. Marvie
HUBIC, Mrs. Vi
KERELUKE, Mrs. Dora
KLOPOUSHAK, Mrs. Eileen
KORPAN, Mrs. Mary
KORPUS, Mrs. Evelyn
KORPUS, Mrs. Sonia
KOSHMAN, Mrs. Mary
KOSHMAN, Mrs. Diana
KOSHOWSKI, Mrs. Nettie
KOWALCHUK, Mrs. Myrtle
KOTYK, Mrs. Annie
KUCEY, Mrs. Eleanor
KUSHNIR, Mrs. Jean
KUSHNIR, Mrs. Marilyn
LAPCHUK, Mrs. Dora
LOZOWCHUK, Mrs. Olenka
LUBY, Mrs. Francis
LUCIUK, Mrs. Cathy
LUZECKY, Mrs. Anne
LYSEIKO, Mrs. Elaine
MAKOWSKY, Mrs. Shirley
MARCHUK, Mrs. Lena
MARUNCHAK, Mrs. Tetiana
MARKO, Mrs. Kathrene
MARUSIAK, Mrs. Sophie
MASLUK, Mrs. Mary

MELNYK, Mrs. Mary
MILLER, Mrs. Carol
MILLER, Mrs. Nellie
MONITA, Mrs. Rosalyn
OSTRYZNIUK, Mrs. Natalie
OZIRNEY, Mrs. Olga
PACHOLEK, Mrs. Sonja
PALYGA, Mrs. Anastasia
PALYGA, Mrs. Anne
PANKIW, Mrs. Rose
PARFENIUK, Mrs. Lena
PASIEKA, Mrs. Kay
PATRYLUK, Mrs. Helen
PATRYLUK, Mrs. Olyne
PAWLUST, Mrs. Mary
PILLIPOW, Mrs. Aileen
POLOWICK, Mrs. Anne
PAWCHUK, Mrs. Elsie
PROCYK, Mrs. Linda
PROCYK, Mrs. Pearl
PROCYSHYN, Mrs. Mary
PROKOPCHUK, Mrs. Rose
SAWCHYN, Mrs. Jean
SEMBALUK, Mrs. Lillian
SENYK, Ms. Natalie
SENYK, Mrs. Sandra
SHIPLACK, Mrs. Eunice
SHIPLACK, Mrs. Lisa
SHIPLACK, Mrs. Peggy
SHIPLACK, Ms. Sylvia
SHISHKOWSKI, Mrs. Eva
SOLTYS, Mrs. Marie
SOPIWNYK, Mrs. Vicky
SORACHAN, Mrs. Mary
STADNYK, Cheryl
STARZYNSKI, Mrs. Helen
STRONSKI, Mrs. Gloria
STURBY, Marilyn
SUPYNUK, Mrs. Anna
SYRNYK, Mrs. Darcy
SYRNYK, Miss Marie
USICK, Mrs. Mary
WARNYCA, Mrs. Agnes
WARNYCA, Mrs. Gwen
WAWRUCK, Mrs. Adele
WELYKHOLOWA, Mrs. Anne
WIWCHAR, Mrs. Lena
ZALESCHUK, Mrs. Anne
ZALESCHUK, Reverend Michael
ZALUSKY, Mrs. Rose
ZENCHYSHYN, Mrs. Nell
ZENZELUK, Mrs. Helen
ZUBKOW, Mrs. Stella

Index

For a Special Gift

An affordable gift idea for friends and family. Please send me _____copies of *Ukrainian Daughters' Cookbook* at $12.95 per book, plus $4.00 (total order) for shipping and handling.

Number of books _____ x $12.95 = $ _____

Postage and handling _____ = $ _____4.00_____

Total enclosed _____ = $ _____

    U.S. and international orders payable in U.S. funds./Price is subject to change.

Name _____

Street_____

City _____Prov./State_____

Country_____Postal Code/Zip _____

Please make cheque or money order payable to: **Ukrainian Women's Association**
                                                                 1920 Toronto Street
                                                                 Regina, Saskatchewan
                                                                 Canada   S4P 1M8

For fund raising or volume purchases, contact Ukrainian Women's Association for volume rates.

For a Special Gift

An affordable gift idea for friends and family. Please send me _____copies of *Ukrainian Daughters' Cookbook* at $12.95 per book, plus $4.00 (total order) for shipping and handling.

Number of books _____ x $12.95 = $ _____

Postage and handling _____ = $ _____4.00_____

Total enclosed _____ = $ _____

    U.S. and international orders payable in U.S. funds./Price is subject to change.

Name _____

Street_____

City _____Prov./State_____

Country_____Postal Code/Zip _____

Please make cheque or money order payable to: **Ukrainian Women's Association**
                                                                   1920 Toronto Street
                                                                 Regina, Saskatchewan
                                                                 Canada   S4P 1M8

For fund raising or volume purchases, contact Ukrainian Women's Association for volume rates.